Effective Writing for Sociology

Writing well is an essential skill for sociologists, but few books help students learn to write well. Designed to help students produce a manuscript that is clear, concise, and compelling, *Effective Writing for Sociology* demonstrates and deconstructs what makes effective writing and how best to communicate scholarly ideas.

The first half of the book addresses the fundamentals of good writing: writing clearly, conveying emphasis, writing concisely, and crafting effective paragraphs. The second half then looks to the three most important sections of a research report: framing an introduction, reporting results, and discussing findings. Each chapter of the book describes strategies for effective writing, illustrated with multiple examples and providing exercises where students can try their hand at implementing these strategies. The Epilogue provides tips on choosing a title as well as writing an abstract and method section; it also includes suggestions on how to master the tips described in the lessons.

Ben Lennox Kail and Robert V. Kail's book is essential reading in courses on research methods, qualitative methods, quantitative methods, sociological writing, and social science writing in allied disciplines such as education, criminology, health, and all research fields.

Ben Lennox Kail is an Associate Professor in Sociology at Georgia Stata University. He earned his undergraduate degree in sociology at IUPUI and did his graduate studies in sociology at Florida State University. After completing his PhD, he spent two years as a NIH Postdoctoral Fellow at Duke University in the demography of aging. Since 2015, he has been an Editorial Board Member of the *Journal of Gerontology: Social Sciences*. He has written 28 peer reviewed papers, as well as several other published papers, chapters, and reports. His research has been featured in various media outlets including local affiliates of Fox, NPR, CBS, as well as nationally on *Today* and in the *New York Times*.

Robert V. Kail is Distinguished Professor Emeritus of Psychological Sciences at Purdue University and Visiting Professor of Psychology at the University of Michigan. His undergraduate degree is from Ohio Wesleyan University, and his PhD is from the University of Michigan. He was named the Distinguished Sesquicentennial Alumnus in Psychology by Ohio Wesleyan University, is a fellow of the Association for Psychological Science, and is an honorary professor at the University of Heidelberg, Germany.

Effective Writing for Sociology

A Guide for Researchers and Students

Ben Lennox Kail and Robert V. Kail

Routledge
Taylor & Francis Group

NEW YORK AND LONDON

Cover image: "200mm", iStock

First published 2023
by Routledge
605 Third Avenue, New York, NY 10158

and by Routledge
2 Park Square, Milton Park, Abingdon, Oxon, OX14 4RN

Routledge is an imprint of the Taylor & Francis Group, an informa business

Library of Congress Cataloging-in-Publication Data
Names: Kail, Ben Lennox, author. | Kail, Robert V., author.
Title: Effective writing for sociology: a guide for researchers and
    students/Ben Lennox Kail and Robert V. Kail.
Description: New York, NY: Routledge, 2022. |
Includes bibliographical references and index.
Identifiers: LCCN 2022019945 | ISBN 9781032357409 (hardback) |
ISBN 9781032357270 (paperback) | ISBN 9781003328285 (ebook)
Subjects: LCSH: Sociology–Authorship. | Sociology–Research. |
    Sociology–Methodology.
Classification: LCC HM569.K35 2022 | DDC 301.072–dc23/eng/20220520
LC record available at https://lccn.loc.gov/2022019945

ISBN: 978-1-032-35740-9 (hbk)
ISBN: 978-1-032-35727-0 (pbk)
ISBN: 978-1-003-32828-5 (ebk)

DOI: 10.4324/9781003328285

Typeset in Garamond
by Deanta Global Publishing Services, Chennai, India

Contents

Acknowledgments

In 2011 Robert V. Kail completed a five-year term as editor of *Psychological Science*, the flagship journal of the Association for Psychological Science. During that editorship, RVK read many manuscripts that were models of effective writing—clear and concise with an important take-home message. But he also read several papers that fell short of this mark: they were wordy, not concise; confusing, not clear; and obscure, not direct. These manuscripts led him to write *Scientific Writing for Psychology*, a brief book containing lessons on how to write effective research reports for psychology.

As a graduate student, Ben Lennox Kail was fortunate to take two classes focused on writing for social sciences. In spring of 2020, BLK began teaching a graduate course on writing for sociology. In this course, he used RVK's *Scientific Writing for Psychology*. The students enjoyed the book, but were occasionally confused because (a) writing for psychology is sufficiently different from writing for sociology that there were a lot of questions about "well, what about ..." and (b) because the substance of the exercises was drawn from psychological research. BLK overcame these obstacles by providing the bridging information between the two disciplines but he realized that someone familiar with both sociology and psychology would be necessary for sociology students to get the most out of *Scientific Writing for Psychology*. BLK mentioned this to RVK and half-joked that they should collaborate on a parallel book for sociology. RVK concurred, and the seed for what would become this book was planted.

Many folks have encouraged our interest in writing and provided us with tips for making our writing more engaging and more inviting. We thank Anne Barrett, Dawn Carr, John Hagen, Harriett Prentiss, Jill Quadagno, and Harold Stevenson. We're also grateful to Dean Birkenkamp for his enthusiastic support of this book from the outset, to the team at Deanta Global Publishing Services for cleaning our prose, and to Helen Birchall, the production editor for shepherding the project to completion.

Finally, we thank our wives (Dea and Christina) whose love and support made this work possible. We also acknowledge each other and are grateful to have had the opportunity to collaborate: we've been family since BLK was born in 1978, but the opportunity to write this book together has added professional icing to the cake that is our relationship. We would also be remiss not to thank you—the reader; writing can be a lot of different things, but this kind of writing is meant to be read. We're glad you're here and grateful that you chose to read this.

Ben Lennox Kail
Robert V. Kail

Prologue

Sociologists need to write well to communicate findings from their research. But training in sociology typically includes few opportunities to master this skill. Undergraduate sociology majors are generally first exposed to scientific writing in a research methods course, where they often write reports of research conducted in class. Some undergraduates later write a senior thesis, and as graduate students they write a master's thesis or a doctoral dissertation. These are all valuable experiences, but they are insufficient to become master writers. After all, athletes or musicians with similar levels of experience are considered novices; they've just started the long trip to mastery.

Our goal in this book is to help you write more effectively. We view effective writing as a craft, a view that has two implications for the book. First, as in most crafts, expert writers often know "tools of the trade"—strategies, tips, heuristics—that make their writing seem clear, concise, cohesive, and compelling. This book is designed to teach you some of these tools that expert authors use to write well.

Second, like most crafts, learning to write well requires massive amounts of practice—10,000 hours is commonly cited as the amount of practice needed to become an expert in many domains. This book includes exercises that allow you to practice these skills without having to wait for your next "official" writing task.

Research reports are among the most important documents that sociologists write: they describe findings that make up the empirical basis of modern scientific sociology and they are the focus of this book. We include seven lessons: three devoted to sentences, one to paragraphs, and three to writing research reports. In each lesson, we describe tools that experts use to write effective sentences, paragraphs, and reports. Additionally, each lesson includes exercises that allow you to try out the tools and ends with "For Practice," which suggests ways to improve your writing by looking at strengths and weaknesses of published articles.

The book ends with an epilogue that provides some finishing touches as well as tips for organizing your writing. This is not a book to be read in one sitting; the book's real value for you is in doing the exercises. Just as athletes master skills by practicing them (not by reading about them), you need to do the exercises to improve your writing. Enough said—let's begin.[1]

Note

1 Throughout the book we use contractions because we want you to feel as if we're talking casually about writing. But don't use contractions in your scientific writing because they're usually considered too informal.

Lesson I

Writing Clearly

Lesson Outline

- What makes some writing hard to read?
- Strategies for writing clear, direct sentences
- Writing long sentences clearly

One sunny afternoon as you're walking to your favorite sociology class, you see a friend. You ask them what they did for lunch today. Imagine that they said the following:

(1a)   After my yoga class, I had my usual lunch: a quinoa salad, an apple, and a cappuccino.

Alternatively, they might have described lunch like this:

(1b)   After completion of my instructional session devoted to physical activity and mental meditation, consumption of a quinoa salad, an apple, and a cappuccino was accomplished by me.

Had they written sentence 1b you probably would have thought them strange (and maybe you would have reconsidered the friendship). Yet when writers move from writing about lunch to writing about sociology, too often they abandon the straightforward style of sentence 1a in favor of the stilted text of sentence 1b.

Consider this pair of sentences:

(2a)   The demonstration of the influence of inequality on social mobility is the primary contribution of this report.

(2b)   Our primary finding is that inequality influences whether and how much families are mobile socially.

DOI: 10.4324/9781003328285-1

Sentence 2a is the sort of sentence that's common in reports published in sociology journals, but sentence 2b expresses the same idea in language that's more direct and easier to understand.
Similarly, compare sentences 3a and 3b.

(3a) Utilization by employers of a college degree as a proxy for cognitive competence is common because this information is easy to obtain.

(3b) Employers often use a college degree as a proxy for cognitive competence because they can obtain this information easily.

The idea that's obscure in sentence 3a is crystal clear in sentence 3b.

In this lesson we'll see how to write sentences like 1a, 2b, and 3b, which are clear, concrete, and direct. We'll also see how to avoid sentences like 1b, 2a, and 3a, which are vague, abstract, and obscure. We'll start by looking at a primary symptom of obscure writing and then consider strategies for writing clearly.

What Makes Some Writing Hard to Read?

Sentences 1b, 2a, and 3a represent a kind of writing that's often known as *bureaucratese* or *academese*, depending on the author's profession. The hallmark of such writing is the frequent presence of **nominalizations,**[1] nouns derived from verbs or adjectives. For example, *organization, utilization, violence,* and *ethnicity* are nominalizations derived from verbs (*organize, utilize*) and adjectives (*violent, ethnic*). Other nominalizations found frequently in sociological writing are shown in Table 1.1.

Nominalizations make writing obscure because they take the concrete action of a verb or the descriptive power of an adjective and bury it in a noun. Nominalizations are particularly detrimental when they appear as the subject of a sentence, coupled with a weak verb, such as *is, are, seems,* or *has.* Sentence 3a illustrates this pattern: "Utilization ... is ... "

Exercise 1.1

Identify the nominalizations in sentences 1b, 2a, and 3a.

Table 1.1 Common Nominalizations

Verb	Nominalization	Adjective	Nominalization
expect	expectation	precise	precision
perform	performance	clear	clarity
evaluate	evaluation	significant	significance
integrate	integration	different	difference

A key to clear writing is recognizing nominalizations and, when possible, returning them to their original state as a verb or adjective. In fact, eliminating unnecessary nominalizations may be the single most important step in making your writing more direct and clearer.

Strategies for Writing Clear, Direct Sentences

Avoiding nominalizations is good advice but not particularly satisfying because it says "what not to do" instead of "what to do." Let's return to sentences 1a and 1b (page 1). Sentence 1b is difficult because of the nominalizations, but it's not the mere absence of nominalizations that makes sentence 1a so easy to understand. Instead, sentence 1a is clear because it's a one-sentence story about a person (your friend) and their actions (eating lunch). As stories go, it's not much; Steven Spielberg isn't about to call for the movie rights. But it's a story nonetheless, and, like much better stories by Zadie Smith, Octavia Butler, and Lee Child, it's readable because it focuses on a person acting.

Storytelling may seem far removed from writing for sociology, but when sociologists write they usually have a tale to tell. Sentence 4a is written in academese:

(4a)   The belief of in-groups is that out-group members are less intelligent and less attractive.

It has a nominalization in its subject (*belief*) that's linked to a weak verb (*is*). But there's a story lurking underneath, one about in-groups and what they believe. Consequently, we get something that's much clearer if we revise the sentence by placing actors in the grammatical subject and their actions in the verb:

(4b) In-groups believe that out-group members are less intelligent and less attractive.

Sentences 5a and 5b show the same pattern:

(5a) Exposure to prescription opioids in a household increases the likelihood of requests for prescription opioids by other family members.

(5b) When individuals are exposed to family members who use prescription opioids, they are more likely to request prescription opioids themselves.

Sentence 5b is easier to read because it puts actors in the subject and changes one nominalization to an adjective (*exposure→exposed*) and the other to a verb (*requests*, a noun→*request*, a verb).

Exercise 1.2

In each sentence, first identify the nominalization, then revise with actions as verbs and actors as subjects.

1. Frequent encounters with aggressive policing lowers African American boys' scores on achievement tests.
2. The cognitive aspects of household labor were the focus of our research.
3. Appropriation of social ties is a common strategy for workers investigating welfare fraud.
4.* Job performance is greater when workers build coalitions with coworkers.[2]

The examples we've seen so far involve simple sentences that include little more than a subject, verb, and object. But the same principles follow when we move to more complex sentences that include, for example, **dependent clauses** like the one in sentence 6a:

(6a) Although adoption of a novel issue by a social movement can enhance recruitment of new members, such diversification of mission often creates conflict within movements.

Sentence 6a begins with a long dependent clause about social movements adopting new issues and then moves to the **independent clause** about the pitfalls of this approach. At the heart of each clause is a noun phrase built around a nominalization: *adoption of a novel issue* and *diversification of mission*. We can make the sentence more active—and clearer— by revising to eliminate the nominalizations, replacing *adoption* with *adopt* and *diversification* with *diversify*:

(6b)   Although social movements that adopt new issues can recruit new members, when social movements diversify, they often experience conflict.

Sentence 7a is similarly complex:

(7a)   Given this inability to identify the influence of immigration on support for welfare spending, the present longitudinal investigation was conducted.

In this case, the introductory dependent clause has two nominalizations (*inability, influence* as a noun), and the independent clause has one (*investigation*). By replacing them with verbs and adjectives, and adding actors for the verbs, the sentence becomes clearer.

(7b)   Because past research has been unable to determine whether immigration influences support for welfare spending, we investigated this issue longitudinally.

When you run into sentences that are even longer and more complex grammatically, the same approach works: find nominalizations, replace them with verbs or adjectives, and add actors to the verbs. That said, although sentences 6b and 7b may be improved over sentences 6a and 7a, they're far from being straightforward. In the next section we'll look at strategies for writing long sentences clearly.

Writing Long Sentences Clearly

Good storytelling focuses on actors and their actions: good sentences get to actors quickly and link those actors strongly with their actions. To translate this principle into a tool for revising, remember that actors are typically introduced in the subject of a sentence; their actions are captured in the verb (and the objects of that verb). This leads directly to one rule of thumb: *effective sentences get to the subject quickly; they do not begin with long introductory clauses that force the reader to wonder what a sentence is about.* Long clauses make sentences 6b and 7b hard to understand. For example, in 6b, the story is about the potential risks when a social movement adds issues, yet the reader must plow through a long clause about the potential benefits. Similarly, in sentence 7b the story is about the author's longitudinal study, but this surfaces only after a lengthy critique of the state of the literature.

If an introductory clause has more than five or six words, shorten it so that the reader gets to the actors sooner. For example, the introductory clause in 6c has only 4 words, down from 12 in 6b.

(6c)   By adopting new issues, social movements can recruit new members but they may experience conflict.

Another strategy is to eliminate the introductory clause completely, by moving it to the end of the sentence:

(7c)   We investigated this issue longitudinally because past research has been unable to determine whether immigration influences support for welfare spending.

Exercise 1.3

Revise these sentences to eliminate the long introductory clause.

1. Because women often compare their income with other women who are also underpaid (relative to men), they may consider this underpayment to be fair.
2. Although the impact of parental income on children's education and their income as adults is well established, less is known concerning the impact of grandparents' wealth on children's outcomes.
3. Given that politicians' attitudes are most influenced by protests involving large numbers of people who convey a unified, straightforward message, organizers should avoid small protests that include divergent voices.
4.* When couples reveal their feelings, address threats to their relationship, and rejoice in each other's accomplishments, their relationship grows stronger.

A second rule of thumb is to *move directly from subject to verb to object; unnecessary words inserted between the subject and verb or between verb and object weaken the links between the key elements in the story line.* Sentence 8a demonstrates this problem:

(8a)   Privileged and marginalized groups, due to different cultures and practices, sometimes struggle to work together effectively.

The story is about groups that try to work together. The actor, *privileged and marginalized groups*, is the subject of the sentence, and the action, *struggle to work together effectively*, is the verb phrase. But inserting *due to different cultures and practices* between subject and verb separates the actor from the actions. Fixing this one is easy:

(8b)   Due to different cultures and practices, privileged and marginalized groups sometimes struggle to work together effectively.

Due to different cultures and practices works fine as an introductory clause because it's only six words long. Removing it from the independent clause strengthens the link between the subject and verb.

Phrases inserted between verbs and objects are just as disruptive:

(9a)   Older adults living in squalor often experience, in all regions of the US, social isolation and conflicted relationships.

The story line about the impact of living in squalor is interrupted by a phrase, *in all regions of the US*, that deals with the generality of the phenomenon. Here, too, moving the phrase to the beginning of the sentence solves the problem:

(9b)   In all regions of the US, older adults living in squalor often experience social isolation and conflicted relationships.

Exercise 1.4

Identify and relocate the disruptive text.

1.   Most newspaper articles about immigrant-related crime, from 1990 to 2014, depicted immigrants as particularly likely to commit crimes.

2. Parents choosing a school for their children, like adults buy-
    ing a car, narrow the options to a manageable number, then
    evaluate each of those options carefully.
3. Part-time employment often involves, especially for Black or
    Hispanic employees, shifts cancelled with little notice or clos-
    ing shifts paired with opening shifts.
4.* Competition between groups, according to this theory, led
    individuals to acquire their group's norms.

Sometimes long sentences aren't clear because they sprawl. Despite a
solid core in which subject, verb, and object are linked well, the sentence goes on and on. One clause is piled on top of another, almost as
if the author kept adding new thoughts while writing. Sentence 10a
illustrates sprawl:

(10a) Widowed older adults are often lonely, which can lead them
       to be depressed, but volunteering can reduce these feelings of
       loneliness.

The sentence starts fine, with a story about a link between widowhood
and loneliness. But then it sprawls as it mentions a consequence of loneliness and then mentions the benefits of volunteering.[3]

The first step in eliminating sentence sprawl is to remember the
storyline and drop text that doesn't contribute. In sentence 10a, the
remark about the benefits of volunteering could be saved for another
sentence:

(10b) Widowed older adults are often lonely, which can lead them to be
       depressed.

Sentence 10b is better but can be improved further. To see how, we need
to focus on *which*, a **relative pronoun** that, like any pronoun, needs a
referent. In sentences such as 10b, the referent of *which* is sometimes
not obvious and readers must search for it, a process that delays their
comprehension momentarily. A trick for handling such sentences is to
replace *which* with its referent and the word *that*. For example, sentence
11a includes a dependent clause that begins with *which*:

(11a) Couples use many strategies to reduce conflicts between work and family, which typically involve women cutting back on work or quitting entirely.

We can replace *which* with its referent—*strategies*—and *that*:

(11b) Couples use many strategies to reduce conflicts between work and family, strategies that typically involve women cutting back on work or quitting entirely.

In 11b, the clause leads with *strategies*, so the reader avoids the ambiguity of *which*. In other words, the repeated noun (*strategies*) anchors the clause, telling readers where they're headed. In the process, it avoids a sprawling sentence that seems to have no direction.

Sentences 12a and 12b illustrate the shortcomings of introducing a clause with *which* and the benefits of replacing *which* with its referent.

(12a) Some companies that embrace diversity invest in mentoring programs, which often increase the number of women and people of color in management.

(12b) Some companies that embrace diversity invest in mentoring programs, programs that often increase the number of women and people of color in management.

In 12b, we replaced *which* with *programs that*. With this change, the reader immediately knows the topic of the clause and the sentence no longer sprawls.

Sometimes the topic of the dependent clause is such that no single word from the main clause is the referent for *which*. In this case, we use a word or phrase to summarize the relevant part of the main clause.

(13a) Women who expect to encounter sexism are particularly attentive to words that are demeaning to females, which supports claims made by Allport (1954) more than 50 years ago.

In 13a, *which* introduces a clause referring to the result described in the main clause; no noun from that clause can substitute for *which*. Instead, we can summarize that main clause by referring to it as *a result*, *a finding*, *an outcome*, or something similar:

(13b) Women who expect to encounter sexism are particularly attentive to words that are demeaning to females, a finding that supports claims made by Allport (1954) more than 50 years ago.

Replacing *which* with a specific noun or noun phrase reenergizes the
sentence, giving it direction.

Sentences 14a and 14b provide another example:

(14a) All correlations are negative and significantly different than 0,
which indicates that people with less education are more prone
to fatal diseases.

In this case, *which* refers to the pattern of correlations (negative and significant); *an outcome* could be inserted instead:

(14b) All correlations are negative and significantly different than 0, an
outcome that indicates people with less education are more prone
to fatal diseases.

Exercise 1.5

Reduce sentence sprawl by eliminating *which*.

1.   Greater income typically allows families greater access to paid
domestic help and to prepared meals, which often reduces the
time that women devote to housework.
2.   The database also included several countries in South America,
which we dropped because their samples were substantially
smaller.
3.   Gangs strongly identify with their neighborhoods, which
helps to explain why gangs defend their turf so vigorously.
4.* When fathers are incarcerated, mothers often find new partners, which has benefits (e.g., offset the loss of the biolog-
ical father) as well as costs (e.g., family life becomes more
complex).

Sentence sprawl can't be blamed entirely on clauses that begin with
which. Sometimes sentences sprawl when authors make comparisons or
include lists. Sentence 15a illustrates sprawl from a comparison:

(15a) Studies with this paradigm typically find that people view members of their own group as friendly and kind but that out-group members are perceived to be hostile.

Sentence 16a shows sprawl from a list:

(16a) When older adults regularly attend movies, art galleries, and concerts, their life satisfaction scores are higher, they report greater control over their lives, and they enjoy life more.

A good way to reduce the kind of sprawl seen in sentences 15a and 16a is by creating parallel structure—by expressing all the elements in the sentence in the same way, using the same grammatical forms. In sentence 15a, for example, the comparisons are completely inconsistent:

- one comparison involves active voice (*people ... view members of their own group*) and another involves passive voice (*out-group members are perceived*);
- one comparison describes the target group completely (*members of their own group*), but the other uses a shorthand (*out-group members*); and
- one comparison mentions two traits (*friendly, kind*), but the other mentions only one (*hostile*).

By expressing all these comparisons in the same terms, we get a sentence that isn't much shorter than 15a but avoids its sprawl:

(15b) Studies with this paradigm typically find that people view in-group members as friendly and kind but that they perceive out-group members as hostile and cruel.

Sentence 15b is easier to read because the comparisons are expressed using parallel structure: the voice is active, the groups are described with shorthand, and the number of traits is the same.

We could shorten it further by deleting *that they perceive*:

(15c) Studies with this paradigm typically find that people view in-group members as friendly and kind but out-group members as hostile and stingy.

And if you were really pressed for space, just use one trait per group:

(15d) Studies with this paradigm typically find that people view in-group members as friendly but out-group members as hostile.

We can use parallel structure to make sentence 16a flow better and be more concise. The trick with this sentence is to recast all the properties (satisfaction, control, enjoyment) in terms of what older adults report:

(16b) When older adults regularly attend movies, art galleries, and concerts, they report greater satisfaction, greater control, and greater enjoyment with life.

Sometimes sprawl resists all the techniques we've mentioned in the past few pages. In that case, there's no shame in splitting the long, sprawling sentence into two shorter, crisper sentences.

(17a) According to the Job Demands–Resources model, employee burnout is more common when jobs demand constant physical or mental effort, but burnout is less common when jobs are seen as stimulating, challenging, and fulfilling, which explains why engaged employees often describe a hard day's work as satisfying rather than exhausting.

Replacing *which* with *an account that* reduces the sprawl but still leaves a mouthful:

(17b) According to the Job Demands–Resources model, employee burnout is more common when jobs demand constant physical or mental effort, but burnout is less common when jobs are seen as stimulating, challenging, and fulfilling, an account that explains why engaged employees often describe a hard day's work as satisfying rather than exhausting.

It's time to surrender and split the sentence in two:

(17c) According to the Job Demands–Resources model, employee burnout is more common when jobs demand constant physical or mental effort, but burnout is less common when jobs are seen as stimulating, challenging, and fulfilling. This account explains why engaged employees often describe a hard day's work as satisfying rather than exhausting.

When you split a sentence in this manner, consider using a semicolon to link the two independent clauses, like this:

(17d) According to the Job Demands–Resources model, employee burnout is more common when jobs demand constant physical or mental effort, but burnout is less common when jobs are seen as stimulating, challenging, and fulfilling; this account explains why engaged employees often describe a hard day's work as satisfying rather than exhausting.

The semicolon is a subtle cue to the reader that the two independent clauses are linked.

Exercise 1.6

Reduce the sprawl in these sentences by rewriting in parallel structure or as two sentences.

1. A "wage penalty" is typical for lower-income mothers because they work fewer hours whereas missing out on job-related experiences often causes higher-income mothers to experience a wage penalty.
2. Adults who attend religious services frequently are more satisfied with their life because they make important friendships from attending services and because these services foster their religious identity.
3. Research on attitudes in the US toward same-sex marriage shows that opposition to same-sex marriage is greater in counties where relatively few women are in the workforce and that crime rate is positively correlated with opposition to same-sex marriage.
4.* In the past decades, sex laws have changed worldwide with laws against sodomy and adultery becoming narrower in scope (e.g., penalizing fewer actions) while a larger range of victims and a larger range of offenders became covered by laws against childhood sex abuse and rape.

Wrap Up

1. Eliminate nominalizations by revising sentences to put actors in the subject and their actions in the verb.
2. Get to the subject quickly (avoid long introductory clauses) and don't interrupt the flow of subject–verb–object.
3. Avoid sentence sprawl by replacing *which* with nouns or noun phrases and by describing comparisons and lists in parallel.

For Practice

1. Search an article for nominalizations; replace the ones that you find.
2. Search for long introductory clauses; shorten or eliminate them.
3. Go on a *"which* hunt"—find clauses that begin with *which* and replace *which* with its referent or a noun phrase.

ANSWERS TO EXERCISES[4]

Exercise 1.1

(1b)   After *completion* of my instructional session devoted to physical *activity* and mental *meditation*, *consumption* of a quinoa salad, an apple, and a cappuccino was accomplished by me.

(2a)   The *demonstration* of the *influence* of *inequality* on social *mobility* is the primary *contribution* of this *report*.

(3a)   *Utilization* by employers of a college degree as a proxy for cognitive *competence* is common because this *information* is easy to obtain.

Exercise 1.2

1. nominalization = encounter(s);   actor = African American boys; action = encounter aggressive policing

African American boys who frequently encounter aggressive policing have lower scores on achievement tests.

2. nominalization = focus (as a noun); actor = our research; action = focus (as a verb)

Our research focused on the cognitive aspects of household labor.

3. nominalization = appropriation; actor = workers; action = appropriate

Workers often appropriate social ties to investigate welfare fraud.

Exercise 1.3

1. Women who are underpaid (relative to men) may consider this fair because they compare their income with other women who are also underpaid.
2. Parents' income influences children's education and their income as adults but we do not know whether grandparents' wealth influences children's outcomes.
3. Protest organizers should avoid small demonstrations that include divergent voices because politicians' attitudes are most influenced by protests involving large numbers of people who convey a unified, straightforward message.

Exercise 1.4

1. From 1990 to 2014, most newspaper articles about immigrant-related crime depicted immigrants as particularly likely to commit crimes.
2. Like adults buying a car, parents choosing a school for their children narrow the options to a manageable number, then evaluate each of those options carefully.
3. For part-time workers, especially Black or Hispanic employees, employment often involves shifts cancelled with little notice or closing shifts paired with opening shifts.

Exercise 1.5

1. Greater income typically allows families greater access to paid domestic help and to prepared meals, a situation that often reduces the time women devote to housework.
2. The database also included several countries in South America, countries that we dropped because their samples were substantially smaller.

3. Gangs strongly identify with their neighborhoods, a phenomenon that helps to explain why gangs defend their turf so vigorously.

Exercise 1.6

1. A "wage penalty" is typical for lower-income mothers because they work fewer hours and typical for higher-income mothers because they miss out on job-related experiences.
2. Adults who attend religious services frequently are more satisfied with their life because attending services helps them make important friendships and fosters their religious identity.
3. Research on attitudes in the US toward same-sex marriage shows that opposition to same-sex marriage is greater in counties where relatively few women are in the workforce and where the crime rate is relatively high.

Notes

1   Technical terms appear in **boldface** and are defined in the Glossary that begins on page 134.
2   Items marked with an asterisk (*) do not have answers listed at the end of the chapter; they are included so that instructors may assign them as homework.
3   By analogy, we can be grateful that the story of the three little pigs wasn't written like this: "The third little pig built a house of bricks, which he bought at the local home improvement center, although he could have paid less for the bricks online."
4   The sentences we include here and throughout the book are designed to illustrate *possible* answers. Please don't consider your answer "wrong" if it doesn't match ours word for word. Your sentence may be better than ours!

Writing with Emphasis

Lesson Outline

- Conveying emphasis through word choice
- Conveying emphasis through sentence structure

In your texts or posts on social media, you probably have emphasized certain parts with capital letters, special fonts, or asterisks. In writing for sociology, we often want to emphasize critical ideas, outcomes, or arguments; but rather than relying on caps, fonts, or asterisks, we convey emphasis with two techniques: word choice and sentence structure.

Conveying Emphasis through Word Choice

You can emphasize elements of a text by the words you use. Consider these two sentences—identical except for the italicized words:

(1a)   The finding that preterm births in the US are *often* less frequent during Democratic presidencies *is consistent with* the claim that political institutions influence health outcomes.

(1b)   The finding that preterm births in the US are *consistently* less frequent during Democratic presidencies *confirms* the claim that political institutions influence health outcomes.

The second sentence seems more emphatic. Why? First, writing that "preterm births in the US are consistently less frequent" describes a stronger finding than "preterm births in the US are often less frequent." The former implies that preterm births are less frequent in nearly all presidencies, but the latter implies they are less frequent only in some presidencies. Second, writing that this finding "confirms" the claim is a

DOI: 10.4324/9781003328285-2

much bolder statement than writing that the results merely "is consistent with" that claim.

Words such as *consistently* and *confirm* are **intensifiers**—they convey energy, substance, and confidence. As in this example, adverbs are often used as intensifiers (*very, quite, certainly, always*) as are verbs (*show, confirm, establish*) and adjectives (*key, crucial, essential, major*). Intensifiers function like the volume control on a guitar's amplifier, producing a "louder" text designed to ensure a reader doesn't miss a critical point.

Sometimes you may want to achieve the opposite effect: instead of being bold and confident, you may want to be tentative and cautious. **Hedges** serve this function; for example, sentence 1a includes one hedge, *often*. Like intensifiers, hedges come as adverbs (*often, sometimes*), adjectives (*many, some*), and verbs (*suggest, seems*).

Sentence 2a begins with a neutral statement, and sentences 2b and 2c show the impact of adding an intensifier and hedge, respectively.

(2a)   Romantic relationships experience problems when couples deviate from norms for gendered behaviors.

(2b)   Romantic relationships *invariably* experience problems when couples deviate from norms for gendered behaviors.

(2c)   Romantic relationships *occasionally* experience problems when couples deviate from norms for gendered behaviors.

Sentence 2b is bold, describing an ironclad link between problems in relationships and deviations from gendered norms. In contrast, sentence 2c is much softer, describing the link as weak or fleeting.

Exercise 2.1

Identify the hedges and intensifiers in these sentences.

1. Youth who live in economically disadvantaged neighborhoods tend to spend less of their awake time in those neighborhoods.
2. When women attend sexist religious institutions, their health is invariably worse than that of women who attend more inclusive religious institutions.

3. The crucial outcome of this work is that cohabitating unions are more likely to dissolve when the individuals in those unions are less educated.
4. Employers typically use characteristics that can be easily observed (e.g., race) to determine whether an applicant will be a productive employee.
5.* Non-profit organizations sometimes attract more donations when their messaging connects with donors' emotions.

Exercise 2.2

Revise these sentences twice, once by intensifying and once by hedging.

1. White adults support tougher laws when they believe Black people are inclined to violence and crime.
2. Relatively affluent people live in communities with like-minded neighbors.
3. In letters of recommendation, men are described as assertive and extraordinary whereas women are described as helpful but temperamental.
4. The Indian Child Welfare Act defines Indian children not by race but by membership in a tribe.
5.* Many married couples who endorse gender equality divide household tasks along traditional gender lines.

You should choose intensifiers and hedges carefully. Writing that's filled with intensifiers can seem arrogant, a tone many readers find offensive. The three sentences in paragraph 3a are filled with intensifiers:

(3a)   Middle-aged men who are less educated are *invariably* unable to complete activities of daily living such as walking and getting dressed. This relationship *definitely* reflects the impact of conducting manual labor. Less educated men *routinely* do manual labor and this *unfailingly* places them at risk for disability.

Instead of respecting a reader's ability to reflect on a passage and draw reasonable conclusions, authors who write like this seem to be saying to a reader, "Open wide because I'm about to force a conclusion down your throat." So, use intensifiers carefully.

But writing that's replete with hedges is also ineffective. Here's the previous paragraph, with a hedge replacing each intensifier.

(3b)   Middle-aged men who are less educated are *occasionally* unable to complete activities of daily living such as walking and getting dressed. This relationship *might* reflect the impact of conducting manual labor. Less educated men *sometimes* do manual labor and this *could* place them at risk for disability.

Readers also react negatively to this version of the paragraph, but for different reasons. The reader thinks the author is insecure—unwilling to state anything with confidence. And if the author lacks confidence in the writing, why should the reader trust the writing or, for that matter, even bother to read it?

These last two paragraphs underscore the need to balance hedging and intensifying, of finding a voice that is neither arrogant nor apprehensive but instead cautiously confident. As you try to find this voice, one strategy is to start with a draft that includes no hedges or intensifiers; if they are stripped from paragraph 3b, we get this:

(3c)   Middle-aged men who are less educated are unable to complete activities of daily living such as walking and getting dressed. This relationship reflects the impact of conducting manual labor. Less educated men do manual labor and this places them at risk for disability.

You'll notice that, without hedges or intensifiers, the paragraph seems reasonably confident. That's usually true: the absence of hedges typically produces a text that's fairly strong. (Notice that in this last sentence, we hedged three times!) Intensifiers should be added with care because they may change the tone from confident to arrogant. However, adding a hedge or two is often useful because it signals the reader that you've got faith in what you're writing but appreciate that the arguments may not be bulletproof (e.g., a result may be open to another interpretation).

Exercise 2.3

Revise each paragraph twice, once in a cautious voice and again in a bold (but *not* a shove-it-down-your-throat) voice.

1. New technology allows detailed assessment of a worker's productivity (e.g., GPS to assess truck drivers). On simple tasks, technology enhances productivity because workers benefit from straightforward feedback about their performance. However, on complex tasks technology lowers productivity because workers focus on aspects of their performance that are readily assessed by technology and ignore other aspects.

2.* Two factors explain why women outperform men in school but underperform men in the workplace. First, women are excluded from some informal social networks that are essential for professional development. Second, women spend more time mentoring, a service that does not lead to pay increases.

Finally, avoid combining hedges and intensifiers in a way that sends a mixed message to your reader. For example, if you hedge your findings, it's best not to intensify the conclusions you draw from those findings. Be particularly careful to avoid combining hedges and intensifiers in the same sentence (e.g., "these findings definitely suggest" or "the results seem to confirm") as this will definitely confuse your readers. Probably.

Conveying Emphasis through Sentence Structure

A politician giving a speech, a marathoner nearing the finish line, and a salesperson negotiating a deal have something in common: they want to end strong. This same strategy works for conveying emphasis in your writing. You want to conclude a sentence with impact, saving the important, innovative, or provocative points for the end. For example, suppose you wanted to describe the emergence of a new theoretical framework. You might write the following:

(4a)   A powerful theoretical framework for studying the polarization of public opinion is suggested by these findings.

But you emphasize the theoretical framework by putting it at the end of the sentence:

(4b)   These findings suggest a powerful theoretical framework for studying the polarization of public opinion.

Now consider this pair of sentences:

(5a)   Two forms of proactive policing common in economically disadvantaged communities are hot spot policing and stop-and-frisk.

(5b)   Hot spot policing and stop-and-frisk are two forms of proactive policing common in economically disadvantaged communities.

Sentence 5a ends with the two forms of proactive policing, a position of emphasis suggesting that the author will be focusing on those specific forms. In contrast, sentence 5b ends with proactive policing in economically disadvantaged communities, a change that leads the reader to expect more about the general nature of this phenomenon.

Let's look at some techniques for ending sentences with a bang, not a whimper.

Cut Unnecessary Material at the End of a Sentence

Consider this:

(6a)   African Americans and Whites who seek employment are equally likely to rely on their social networks, which include family, friends, and, occasionally, neighbors.

The important claim here is job seekers' use of social networks. The phrase "which include family, friends, and, occasionally, neighbors" seems like an afterthought that contributes nothing to the main point of the sentence. Eliminating that phrase puts the emphasis where it belongs, on *use* of social networks to find employment.

(6b)   African Americans and Whites who seek employment are equally likely to rely on their social networks.

Here's another example:

(7a)   In the US, parents who decline vaccines for their children tend to be White, well educated, and well paid as measured in dollars.

This sentence ends weakly because of the phrase "as measured in dollars." The phrase is unnecessary because most people in the US are paid in dollars. Without the phrase, the sentence ends strongly, with the three characteristics that define American parents who decline vaccines for their children:

(7b)   In the US, parents who decline vaccines for their children tend to be White, well educated, and well paid.

Exercise 2.4

Trim unnecessary words to create greater emphasis.

1. When people are affluent and physically safe, they are more cooperative with other people.
2. In the US, undocumented students often struggle to go to college because they are typically ineligible for loans to pay for their education.
3. Auto insurance companies use credit scores to determine whether to insure a driver because such scores predict whether a driver will be in an accident or not be in an accident.
4.* Parents must certify that they are eligible for subsidies by documenting their wages in person or online.

Put Context-Setting Material at the Beginning of a Sentence

Sometimes you may want to put a statement in context. For example, you might want to cite the source of findings that support a claim. Or you might want to indicate that a statement applies broadly, across cultures, domains, or conditions. Such context-setting remarks work better at the beginning of a sentence than at the end. Look at the following pair of sentences:

(8a)   Based on analyses of data from the Behavioral Risk Factor Surveillance System, transgender women who sound like men have better self-reported health than transgender women who sound like women.

(8b) Transgender women who sound like men have better self-reported health than transgender women who sound like women, based on analyses of data from the Behavioral Risk Factor Surveillance System.

The interesting finding here is the link between health and the sound of a transgender woman's voice. Sentence 8a emphasizes that result by placing it at the end of the sentence. In contrast, sentence 8b starts with the interesting result but ends weakly by specifying the source of the data producing the result.

The next pair of sentences shows the same pattern:

(9a) In France, Germany, and the United States, workers tend to earn more when their jobs match their level of education.
(9b) Workers tend to earn more when their jobs match their level of education, in France, Germany, and the United States.

Sentence 9a gets the information about countries out of the way and finishes with impact by emphasizing the link between earnings and the match between jobs and education. In contrast, sentence 9b leads with that interesting result but then ends inconsequentially by mentioning the countries where that result is observed.

There is an important exception to the rule of putting context-setting information at the beginning of a sentence: sometimes information about context is to be emphasized, which means it should appear at the end of the sentence, not the beginning. For example, sentence 8b might be preferred over sentence 8a if the critical idea is that link between health and the sound of a transgender woman's voice is based on one set of data and should be replicated. Similarly, sentence 9b would work better than sentence 9a if the goal were to establish that link between earnings and the match between jobs and education is found in countries other than the US.

Exercise 2.5

Revise each sentence so that the context-setting material in italics appears at the beginning of the sentence.

1. Workers feel unhappy and distressed when their work schedules are unstable, *based on findings from hourly workers in the service industry.*

2. Students from economically disadvantaged families frequently lack the social capital needed to succeed in school and to prepare for college, *according to Boudon's framework.*

3. Well-educated people are not as likely as less-educated people to have ever smoked regularly, *although this effect is weaker in people born before 1960.*

4.* Black immigrants' earnings rarely catch up to those of native Whites, *as is true for Hispanic immigrants.*

Move Important Elements toward the End of the Sentence

Sometimes you want to move words toward the end of a sentence so they receive the emphasis they deserve. Here are two techniques to do this:

1. Insert *there/it/what* + a verb (usually a form of *to be*, such as *is*, *are*, *was*, or *were*):

Sentence 10a is clear but lacking in punch.

(10a) Low-income Americans are typically not very active politically.

In 10a, the important ideas are distributed across the entire sentence: *low-income Americans* is the subject's sentence and *are typically not very active politically* is the verb phrase. In contrast, 10b is strong because all these ideas are moved closer to the end of the sentence:

(10b) There is compelling evidence that low-income Americans are typically not very active politically.

Similarly, sentence 11a is clear but weak:

(11a) Beyond adolescence, the marketplace drives segregation by gender.

But starting the sentence with "What is striking is that" puts the critical information closer to the end of the sentence:

(11b) What is striking is that, beyond adolescence, the marketplace drives segregation by gender.

Finally, sentence 12b uses "It is" to achieve greater emphasis:

(12a) Violent young men threaten their girlfriends to not use contraception.
(12b) It is noteworthy that violent young men threaten their girlfriends to not use contraception.

Use these techniques sparingly, saving them for sentences that demand emphasis. Why? First, these techniques contradict the advice from Lesson 1: that sentences have subjects and verbs that are specific and descriptive. "It is" and "there are" are hollow (one reason why some teachers and editors suggest writers avoid them altogether). Second, they make sentences longer, which goes against the goal of writing concisely. Nevertheless, used occasionally, these techniques help draw the reader's attention to a key point.

2.   Add *not only X but Y*

One way to create emphasis is to contrast one element with others. For example, perhaps X is known to affect educational attainment; your work has shown that Y is an additional influence. The *not only X but Y* construction makes this comparison explicit and conveniently puts Y at the emphasis-receiving end of the sentence.

Suppose you've analyzed the factors that contribute to the prestige of an occupation. You find that occupations are judged to be more prestigious when they're associated with high salaries and when they're thought to be important to a community. The former result replicates previous studies, but the latter result is novel. You might write this:

(13a) The prestige of an occupation is based on income and importance to the community.

This sentence is clear but does not highlight the novel result. Using *not only X but Y* makes the novel result stand out:

(13b) The prestige of an occupation is based not only on income but also on importance to the community.

Similarly, if your novel claim is that workers leave the workforce to care for children, you might write this:

(14a) American workers experience a lapse in employment because they lose their job or because they leave work to care for children.

This is clear but does little to sell the novel idea.

(14b) American workers experience a lapse in employment not only because they lose their job but also because they leave work to care for children.

Sentence 14b is more effective because *not only X but Y* contrasts the new idea with the accepted ideas.

Used effectively, *not only X but Y* is a powerful tool for highlighting new information. But many writers use it incorrectly, misplacing *only*. For *not only X but Y* to work, X and Y must be the same part of speech. For example, consider these sentences:

(15a) In our analyses, we controlled not only for GDP per capita but also for ethnic fractionalization.
(15b) In our analyses, we not only controlled for GDP per capita but also for ethnic fractionalization.

Sentence 15a is correct because X and Y are both noun phrases (*GDP per capita, ethnic fractionalization*). Sentence 15b is incorrect because X is a verb phrase (*not only controlled*) but Y is a noun phrase (*ethnic fractionalization*).

Similarly, in this pair of sentences

(16a) Firms that have a good reputation are judged less harshly not only when their products fail but also when their earnings decline.
(16b) Firms that have a good reputation are not only judged less harshly when products fail but also when their earnings decline.

Sentence 16a is correct because X and Y are both **adverbial clauses** (*when their products fail, when their earnings decline*). Sentence 16b is incorrect because X is a verb (*judged*) but Y is a adverbial clause (*when their earnings decline*). So, after you've written a sentence that includes *not only X but Y* be sure to check that X and Y belong to the same grammatical class.

Exercise 2.6

Use the four techniques we've just described to revise each of these sentences so the material to be emphasized is moved closer to the end of the sentence.

1. Mothers receive less pay than women who are not mothers, but the size of the gap depends on a mother's race, her marital status, and her age at first childbirth.
2. When people retire, they less often become depressed if they receive social support from friends.
3. Finding former white supremacists for research is difficult because they rarely identify as such and because they sever all connections with organizations to which they belonged.
4. Non-profit organizations that focus on making stronger communities help to reduce property crime and violent crime.
5.* Big data analytics often integrate conventional criminal data with data obtained from noncriminal settings, a practice that means police have data for individuals who have not had contact with the police.

Wrap Up

1. Use intensifiers to add emphasis and hedges to convey caution. But don't overuse these words: too many intensifiers make your writing seem arrogant and too many hedges make it seem feeble.
2. Put material you want to emphasize at the end of the sentence. Techniques for doing this include eliminating unnecessary words, putting context-setting comments at the beginning of a sentence, and shifting text to the right.

For Practice

1. Identify hedges and intensifiers in a randomly selected paragraph; replace hedges with intensifiers and vice versa.
2. Find sentences that include unnecessary material at the end, material that causes them to end weakly.
3. Find sentences that put context-setting material in an introductory clause. Rewrite the sentences to have this material at the end; notice how the emphasis changes.

4. Find sentences that use *that/it/what* for emphasis. Delete this material and note the change in emphasis.
5. Find sentences that list multiple elements; revise using *not only X but Y* to emphasize one element.

ANSWERS TO EXERCISES

Exercise 2.1

1. Youth who live in economically disadvantaged neighborhoods *tend to* [hedge] spend less of their awake time in those neighborhoods.
2. When women attend sexist religious institutions, their health is *invariably* [intensifier] worse than that of women who attend more inclusive religious institutions.
3. The *crucial* [intensifier] outcome of this work is that cohabitating unions are more likely to dissolve when the individuals in those unions are less educated.
4. Employers *typically* [hedge] use characteristics that can be easily observed (e.g., race) to determine whether an applicant will be a productive employee.

Exercise 2.2

1. White adults *tend to* support tougher laws when they believe Black people are inclined to violence and crime. [hedge with verb]

All White adults support tougher laws when they believe Black people are inclined to violence and crime. [intensify with adjective]

2. Relatively affluent people *invariably* live in communities with like-minded neighbors. [intensify with adverb]

Relatively affluent people *sometimes* live in communities with like-minded neighbors. [hedge with adverb]

3. In letters of recommendation, men are *consistently* described as assertive and extraordinary whereas women are *almost always* described as helpful but temperamental. [intensify with adverb]

In letters of recommendation, men are *occasionally* described as assertive and extraordinary whereas women are *sporadically* described as helpful but temperamental. [hedge with adverb]

4. The Indian Child Welfare Act defines *all* Indian children not by race but by membership in a tribe. [intensify with adjective]

The Indian Child Welfare Act defines *some* Indian children not by race but by membership in a tribe. [hedge with verb]

Exercise 2.3

Cautious version:

New technology *sometimes* allows detailed assessment of a worker's productivity (e.g., GPS to assess truck drivers). On simple tasks, such technology *occasionally* enhances productivity because workers benefit *often* from straightforward feedback about their performance. However, on complex tasks technology *at times* lowers productivity because workers *intermittently* focus on aspects of their performance that are readily assessed by technology and ignore other aspects.

Bold version:

New technology *usually* allows detailed assessment of a worker's productivity (e.g., GPS to assess truck drivers). On simple tasks, such technology *regularly* enhances productivity because workers *invariably* benefit from straightforward feedback about their performance. However, on complex tasks technology *consistently* lowers productivity because workers *always* focus on aspects of their performance that are readily assessed by technology and ignore other aspects.

Exercise 2.4

1. When people are affluent and physically safe, they are more cooperative ~~with other people~~. [By definition, cooperation involves other people.]
2. In the US, undocumented students often struggle to go to college because they are typically ineligible for loans ~~to pay~~

for their education. [By definition, loans are used to pay for things and it's obvious here that loans would be for education.]

3. Auto insurance companies use credit scores to determine whether to insure a driver because such scores predict whether a driver will be in an accident or not be in an accident. [If scores predict who will be in an accident, that implies they also predict who will not be in an accident.]

Exercise 2.5

1. Based on findings from hourly workers in the service industry, workers feel unhappy and distressed when their work schedules are unstable.
2. According to Boudon's framework, students from economically disadvantaged families frequently lack the social capital needed to succeed in school and to prepare for college.
3. Although the effect is weaker in people born before 1960, well-educated people are not as likely as less-educated people to have ever smoked regularly.

Exercise 2.6

1. It is striking that mothers receive less pay than women who are not mothers, but the size of the gap depends on a mother's race, her marital status, and her age at first childbirth. OR

Mothers receive less pay than women who are not mothers, but the size of the gap depends not only on a mother's race, her marital status, but also on her age at first childbirth.

2. There is compelling evidence that when people retire they less often become depressed if they receive social support from friends. OR

It is noteworthy that when people retire ...

3. What emerges in this literature is that finding former white supremacists for research is difficult because they rarely identify as such and because they sever all connections with organizations to which they belonged. OR

Finding former white supremacists for research is difficult not only because they rarely identify as such but also because they sever all connections with organizations to which they belonged.

4. Non-profit organizations that focus on making stronger communities help to reduce not only property crime but also violent crime. OR

What is noteworthy is that non-profit organizations that focus on making stronger communities help to reduce property crime and violent crime.

Lesson 3

Writing Concisely, with Some Spice

Lesson Outline

- Writing concisely
- Adding spice

Confession time: this lesson is actually two mini-lessons, one about writing concisely and one about adding spice to your writing. Neither topic warrants a full lesson, so we've merged them here. We start with writing concisely.

Writing Concisely

Scientific writing is concise. Why? One reason is that scientists are busy and can't waste time reading wordy reports. A second reason is that many journals limit the number of words they will allow in a manuscript. A third reason—our favorite—is that it's aesthetically satisfying to hit the "sweet spot" on length—just the right number of words for readers to understand a study fully: no more, and no less.

In this half lesson, we mention four tips for concise writing.

Tip #1: Change Negatives to Affirmatives

Most phrases of the form *not* + X can be rewritten in the affirmative:

    not missing → present
    not stop → continue
    not empty → full

DOI: 10.4324/9781003328285-3

Sentence 1a includes such a *not* + *X* phrase:

(1a)   Men in female-typical roles experience less authority than their female counterparts, but this does not last long.

If the *not* + *X* is replaced,

(1b)   Men in female-typical roles experience less authority than their female counterparts, but this lasts briefly.

we use two fewer words. Just as important, the sentence becomes slightly clearer because definitions involving the absence of features (e.g., *not long*) are typically vaguer than those involving the presence of features (e.g., *briefly*). In other words, definitions are more precise when they specify what something is rather than what it is not.

Exercise 3.1

Change the negatives to affirmatives.

1. Our baseline model assumes that patterns of exchange mobility do not change over time.
2. Online social networks could reduce social segregation because adolescents would not be limited to befriending agemates from their school.
3. Moving allows residents to create a new narrative of safety, even when residents do not move far.
4.* Government officials' views are not always stable.

Tip #2: Delete What Readers Can Infer

Writers sometimes include adjectives that are redundant; they're unnecessary because they're implicit in the noun they modify. Examples include *terrible tragedy*, *true facts*, and *future plans*. By definition, tragedies are terrible, facts are true, and plans are for the future. The adjectives are wasted words. Consequently, in this sentence

(2a)   Charities that provide free gifts to children receive more dona-
        tions when requests for donations are expressed in positive
        emotions.

we can delete *free* without any loss in meaning because, by definition,
gifts are free:

(2b)   Charities that provide gifts to children receive more donations
        when requests for donations are expressed in positive emotions.

Similarly, many adverbs are unnecessary because they're implicit in the
verbs they modify. Examples here include *finish completely*, *prove conclu-
sively*, and *suggest tentatively*.
    A related mistake is to include categories that are implied by words.
Examples include *period of time*, *honest in character*, and *depreciate in value*.
In each of these cases, the category (e.g., time, character, value) is implied
by the initial noun, adjective, or verb. In sentence 3a, for example,

(3a)   Previously, organ donation was seen as unusual in nature.

in nature is unnecessary because it's implicit in *unusual*:

(3b)   Previously organ donation was seen as unusual.

This tip, like the previous one, only saves a word or two. But these can
add up over the course of a manuscript.

Exercise 3.2

Delete what readers can infer.

1. The sample is representative, includes multiple indicators of
   race, and is large in size.
2. Of the students who completely finished the academic secondary school track, 53% went to college.
3. Groups sometimes reach consensus of opinion based on the
   attitudes of one influential person.
4.* After being ostracized by others, children reaffiliate with their
   own group.

Table 3.1 Common Phrases That Can Be Replaced by
a Single Word

Phrase	Word
A large percentage of	Most
As a consequence of	Because
At that point in time	Then
At the present time	Now
Due to the fact that	Because
Has a requirement for	Needs
In a timely manner	Promptly
In close proximity to	Near
In some cases	Sometimes
In the near future	Soon
In the situation where	When
Subsequent to	After
With reference to	About
With the exception of	Except

Tip #3: Replace Phrases with Words

English is filled with short phrases that can be replaced with a single word. Table 3.1 lists some illustrative examples, but there are dozens more! For example, in sentence 4a

(4a)   In the event that a parolee misses a scheduled visit with a parole officer, the officer may issue a warrant.

In the event that can be replaced by *if*—saving 3 words (and 15 characters!).

(4b)   If a parolee misses a scheduled visit with a parole officer, the officer may issue a warrant.

Because English has so many phrases like those in Table 3.1, you can't hope to remember them all. Instead, as you edit your writing, pay attention to well-worn phrases. Then see if you can replace them with a single word.

Exercise 3.3

Identify phrases that can be replaced by an individual word.

1. The evidence suggests that neither fertility nor mortality will change in the near future.
2. When people in blended families experience conflict, they have a tendency to blame it on tension related to their children.
3. Immigrants' proficiency in English is determined by several traits acquired during the time they were growing up in their home countries.
4.* The findings suggest that education has an effect on liberal attitudes but not on intergroup conflict or competition.

Tip #4: Delete Adverbs and Adjectives

This may seem like a radical proposal—eliminating two parts of speech! However, too many writers insert adjectives or adverbs that have little meaning. Consequently, a good revision strategy is to create a version of a sentence with no adjectives or adverbs and then reinsert only those essential to the sentence's meaning.

In sentence 5a, the adjectives and adverbs are in italics; in sentence 5b, they've been deleted.

(5a) Interviewers *often* gesture during *routine investigative* interviews, a *nonverbal* behavior that *certainly* affects the interviewee's *vocal* responses.

(5b) Interviewers gesture during interviews, a behavior that affects the interviewee's responses.

One approach is to rank the deleted words in their importance to the sentence. (Of course, the surrounding sentences provide a context that determines the importance of individual words; not knowing that context, our choices are more tentative.) Of the six italicized words (*often, routine, investigative, nonverbal, certainly, vocal*), we would rank *investigative* as the most important; it seems essential because it identifies the setting in which gestures take place. We would rank *routine* and *certainly* as the least important. How does a routine investigative interview differ from one that's nonroutine? *Certainly* is an intensifier that's unnecessary: *behavior that affects the interviewee's responses* is sufficiently strong. *Often* is a hedge; it could be included if the authors want to be cautious regarding their claims. *Nonverbal* and *vocal* might help to emphasize the contrast between different modes of communicative behavior. Our preferred version of the sentence is this:

(5c)   Interviewers *often* gesture during *investigative* interviews, a *nonverbal* behavior that affects the interviewee's *vocal* responses.

Sentence 6a provides another example in which adjectives and adverbs are italicized; in sentence 6b, they've been omitted.

(6a)   When an organization allows members to maintain ties to non-members, it may *actually* grow because recruitment is *really* easier, but it may shrink because members are *very* attracted to *other*, *alternative* organizations.
(6b)   When an organization allows members to maintain ties to non-members, it may grow because recruitment is easier, but it may shrink because members are attracted to organizations.

Of the five deleted words—*actually*, *really*, *very*, *other*, *alternative*—the sentence needs *other* or *alternative*. Either would capture the idea that other (or alternative) organizations may compete for membership. But none of the others contribute. We like sentence 6c:

(6c)   When an organization allows members to maintain ties to non-members, it may grow because recruitment is easier, but it may shrink because members are attracted to *other* organizations.

This delete-all-adjectives-and-adverbs strategy is labor-intensive but worth the effort: In both examples, four words were deleted, producing sentences that were not only shorter but crisper. Until this leaner style of writing comes automatically, one step of your revising might be to delete one adjective (or adverb) from every sentence or five from each paragraph. For some sentences and paragraphs this won't be possible. But most of the time you'll find plenty of excess adjectives and adverbs, a process that will hone your skill in identifying nonessential words. And used with the other strategies mentioned here (change negatives to affirmatives, delete what readers can infer, replace phrases with words), your writing will get closer to that aesthetically pleasing sweet spot-on length.[1]

Exercise 3.4

Identify all the adjectives and adverbs; delete those that are unnecessary.

1. Married individuals who verbally report having a truly happy marriage actually have better physical health and increased longevity.
2. Social class is a meaningful characteristic that generally influences various perceptions of confidence.
3. Children of foreign immigrants typically enter US schools with somewhat limited knowledge of US culture, yet they often are relatively more successful in school than their native-born peers.
4.* Surveillance in affordable subsidized housing creates a home environment that lacks basic privacy and makes residents feel as if they are literally imprisoned.

Adding Spice

We've searched the Internet high and low but can't find a single website that says writing for sociology should be boring. Nevertheless, many writers seem to strive for a style that's clear but so dull that *How to Repair Your Lawnmower* seems riveting by comparison. This is silly; sociology is poorly served when articles make for tedious reading. Sociology is exciting; there's no reason articles shouldn't convey that excitement to the reader. In this mini-lesson, we suggest several tips for spicing up your writing. They won't turn you into a bestselling novelist, but they will help to create a story line that's lively and engaging. What's more, many of these tips will help your readers understand your work and remember your findings.

Tip #5: Writing Actively

In the lesson on writing clearly, we emphasized that sentences are easier to understand when they have actors as subjects and their actions as verbs. That practice also makes your writing more animated and more appealing. As a reminder of the pitfalls of sentences filled with nominalizations, sentence 7a

(7a)   Worldwide, contraceptive use is greatest when it is framed as a matter of women's health.

is no more engaging than a repair manual. But revised to emphasize characters and actions,

(7b)   Women worldwide more often use contraception when they believe it helps them stay healthy.

the sentence comes alive; it's no longer about abstractions but women's actions and beliefs.

Tip #6: Figures of Speech

Skilled writers often enrich their prose with figures of speech—devices in which words are used in special ways to achieve a distinct effect. For example, in **hyperbole** exaggerated statements are used for emphasis. In **understatement**, the description is deliberately weaker than the facts or conditions warrant. Frankly, both hyperbole and understatement are risky for scientific writing because readers may interpret them literally, not figuratively.

Simile and Metaphor

Other figures of speech are more useful. **Simile** and **metaphor** both involve comparing dissimilar objects, typically so the text is clearer or more vivid. In other words, similes and metaphors can aid comprehension by comparing a novel idea or concept with familiar ideas or concepts. For example, sentence 8 refers to the familiar Nike swoosh to indicate the importance of inflation as a measure of economic instability.

(8)   Inflation signifies economic instability, just as the swoosh signifies Nike products.

Similarly, sentence 9 uses birth to introduce factors that create challenges for social movements.

(9)   Social movements must confront the factors that give birth to nonparticipation.

In addition to aiding comprehension, simile and metaphor can make sentences more vivid. They are often handy for emphasizing quantitative phenomena, such as the strength of an effect or the likelihood an outcome. Sentence 10 uses a simile to express how easily a target was detected:

(10) Acts of burglary and auto theft are detected as easily as a red cap on a field of new-fallen snow.

Sentence 11 uses a metaphor to emphasize that an effect was large:

(11) The difference in reading scores between low- and medium-income students represents an industrial-strength effect.

Finally, sentence 12 uses a simile to emphasize that a phenomenon is likely:

(12) Among those working on Wall Street, the breadwinner-home-maker arrangement remains as common as ants at a summer picnic.

Of course, metaphors and similes aren't restricted to size-related comparisons; most ideas can be made more familiar and more interesting with simile and metaphor. You can find scores of websites devoted to metaphors and similes that can inspire you to create your own. As you do, however, be wary of three traps that can snare a novice metaphor writer. (Notice that metaphor?) First, avoid mixed metaphors like the one in sentence 13a.

(13a) Divorce mediators fly high when neither party has legal representation but drown when both parties have legal representation.

The problem is that the sentence begins with a comparison to flying and then shifts to a comparison with swimming. Sentence 13b eliminates this problem by having a constant reference: smooth and difficult sailing.

(13b) Divorce mediators have smooth sailing when neither party has legal representation but encounter choppy water when both parties have legal representation.

However, sentence 13b illustrates a second trap: a cliché. Hundreds (thousands?) of writers have used this comparison (smooth vs. choppy water) before, which makes it less vivid. Sentence 14a has the same problem:

(14a) Bills expanding health care moved through the legislative process at a snail's pace.

Sentence 14b avoids the clichéd comparison:

(14b) Bills expanding health care moved through the legislative process at a pace slower than a checkout line at Target on Black Friday.

Nevertheless, sentence 14b illustrates a third trap: similes and metaphors are effective only when readers understand the reference—in this case, that a checkout line at Target on Black Friday often moves very, very slowly. Readers who aren't familiar with Black Friday[2] (or don't know that Target is a chain of retail stores) will end up confused, not enlightened.

These examples show that the road to a successful metaphor is filled with obstacles.[3] But creating an effective metaphor is worth the effort because it animates your writing and makes it stand out from ordinary scientific text.

Exercise 3.5

Complete the sentence with a simile or metaphor. The words in brackets hint at a basis of comparison.

1. In the United States, COVID-19 raced through African American communities like … [a relay team's last runner].
2. Collective locomotion of the sort that occurs in street actions typically move erratically, like … [novice ship navigator].
3. Released prisoners often report feeling estranged and out of place in civilian life, like … [an unusual instrument in a marching band].
4* The hold of the elite closure model of educational achievement on sociological theorizing is tenacious, like … [an unwanted house guest].

Antimetabole

You may not know another useful figure of speech by name, but you'll likely recognize familiar examples:

(15)   "Ask not what *your country* can do for *you*; ask what *you* can do for *your country*." (John F. Kennedy)

(16)   "We didn't *land* at Plymouth *Rock*. The *rock landed* on us." (Malcolm X)

(17)   "In the end, the true test is not the *speeches* a president *delivers*. It's whether he *delivers* on his *speeches*." (Hillary Clinton)

These examples illustrate **antimetabole**, a figure of speech in which words are repeated, in reverse order. Sentences 15 through 17 illustrate two main properties of antimetabole:

- The repeated words are often nouns or noun phrases.
- The nouns are usually linked by the same word (or words) in both instances.

A first step in creating your own antimetabole is to identify two nouns that refer to key elements in your work. Then think about verbs or phrases that describe how these elements are related in your work. As an example, consider research on people's religious beliefs. This work demonstrates wide-ranging behavioral consequences of belief in God but has done little to clarify the nature of those beliefs. We chose *God* and *belief* as the key nouns and after some experimentation came up with this:

(18)   Thus, research reveals much about the impact of *people's belief* in *God* but tells little about the *God* in *people's beliefs*.

As another example, sentence 19 summarizes findings that show mutual influence of emotional control on the quality of marriage:

(19)   Couples who frequently *control their emotions for the sake of their marriage* sometimes end up *controlling their marriage for the sake of their emotions*.

Creating good antimetaboles is challenging, but they can be remarkably effective, especially as the last sentence of a paper. It's not a coincidence that sentences with antimetabole rank high among the best-known quotations of historical figures.

Exercise 3.6

Finish the sentence with an antimetabole that uses the italicized words and describes the findings in brackets.

1. Social movements are not *innovative* because they are *successful*, instead ... [social movements that yield results tend to have new ideas].
2. When elected officials *lose sight of outcomes*, the likely ... [they probably won't be re-elected].
3. What matters most is *not protecting the wages of workers* who provide *health care* but, instead, ... [the safe keeping of workers without money].
4.* If *leaders* emphasize a group's shared *values*, typically ... [group members think highly of the people in charge of the group].

Tip #7: Creating New Words

Many fiction writers create new words specifically to enliven their storytelling. Shakespeare was an expert, creating more than 1,000 new words (and we can thank him for the always useful *puke*), and modern novelists continue the practice (Plotnik, 2007). Used sparingly and carefully, such **neologisms** can enhance scientific writing, too.

There are many techniques for creating new words, including shortening an existing word (e.g., *prob* for *probably*, *obv* for *obviously*), blending existing words (e.g., *snowmageddon* to refer to a massive snowstorm, *Kimye* to refer to Kim Kardashian and Kanye West), and using the names of well-known people as nouns or verbs (e.g., *Tebowing* to mean dropping to a knee to pray). Here we focus on three other options because they seem the easiest to use and work well with sociological content.

Adding Prefixes and Suffixes

English is filled with prefixes and suffixes; Table 3.2 lists some familiar examples. Adding one of them to an existing word is the simplest way to create a new word. For example, a small-scale protest is a *microprotest*; individuals who thrive on excluding others from social interactions are *excludaholics*.

Table 3.2 Common Prefixes and Suffixes That Can Be Used to Create New Words

Prefix	Meaning	Suffix	Meaning
a (an)-	without	-able	capable of
macro/micro-	large/small	-aholic	one addicted to something
mis-	faulty	-cian/-ee/-er	one who
neo-	new	-ism	belief system
omni-	all, always	-ize	to cause
pseudo-	fake, false	-ness	state of

Exercise 3.7

Combine *tax* with a prefix or suffix from Table 3.2 to make a new word that fits the definition given in each sentence.

1. Something that looks like a *tax* but isn't.
2. To *tax* someone incorrectly.
3. People who *tax* compulsively.
4.* A belief in the virtues of aggressive *taxing*.

Hyperhyphenated Modifiers

English is filled with hyphenated phrases that work as a unit to modify a word, typically a noun. Familiar examples include a *deer-in-the-head-lights* look, a *state-of-the-art* computer, and an *over-the-top* experience. But you can create your own hyphenated phrases, as we did on page 21 in suggesting that you avoid a *shove-it-down-your-throat* voice. Some other examples include *choke-under-pressure* leaders, *aggressive-toward-other-people* dreams, and *short-term-profit-maximizing* investors.

A common situation where hyperhyphenation is useful is a sentence with a long noun phrase, such as sentence 20a:

(20a) Trans women who are barred from female housing illustrate ...

This sentence is difficult because readers must slog through a long phrase before they get to the main verb, *illustrate*. Using hyperhyphenation produces this:

(20b) Barred-from-female-housing trans women illustrate ...

Hyperhyphenation cues the reader that the words should be a unit. Placing them before the noun (as with any adjective) puts the subject and verb of the sentence together. But the main reason for hyperhyphenation is that its very novelty (particularly in writing for sociology) highlights the hyphenated words and, in the process, adds some zip to your text.

Before you go wild with hyperhyphenation, we offer some warnings. First, don't use a hyperhyphenated phrase when an existing adjective would fit perfectly. If you write *have-abundant-material-possessions people* instead of *affluent people*, readers will think that either your vocabulary is limited or you're showing off. Second, be particularly careful when using hyperhyphenated phrases to describe people because this can be dehumanizing (i.e., it equates the person with the description and makes the person nothing more than a group member). In other words, people with many material possessions are not just wealthy; they may also be friendly, happy, or irresponsible. Referring to them as *affluent people* reduces them to a single dimension and makes the group seem more homogeneous than it is. Third, avoid *Hey!-look-what-I-can-do-with-lots-of-hyphens-in-my-writing-to-get-your-undivided-attention* phrases. As a rule of thumb, hyperhyphenated phrases are probably most effective when they include three to five words.

Exercise 3.8

Hyperhyphenate to create a phrase that modifies the italicized noun.

1. The *motive* to perceive the social system as fair is particularly well established ...
2. The findings help to explain the prevalence of *evangelicals* who take offense at TV news.
3. *Families* who are seeking forever homes take their time to find homes that meet their ideal homes and neighborhoods.
4.* Compared with workers in socialist countries, workers in capitalist countries more often use career *strategies* that emphasize promotion and advancement.

Verbing

Fifty years ago, *dialogue, impact*, and *message* were used only as nouns, but today each is often used as a verb.

(21)   Effective bosses frequently *dialogue* with their employees.

(22)   The aim of our research was to determine how neighborhood disadvantage can *impact* college outcomes.

(23)   On dating websites, bisexual adults typically *message* either males or females, not both.

Such **verbing** is most effective when the meaning of the new verb is novel and obvious. The well-known *google* fits these criteria. So does *podium*, as in *the relay team hopes to podium in the upcoming Olympic games.*

To do your own verbing, search for nouns. You'll discover that many don't qualify because they already have verb forms. (Remember, this is how nominalizations are created, by making a noun from a verb or adjective.) Good candidates are often nouns that serve as objects of verbs. For example, in sentence 24a *rapport* is the object of *developed*:

(24a)   Through repeated interviews, we developed *rapport* with participants.

In sentence 24b, it's a new verb:

(24b)   Through repeated interviews, we *rapported* with participants.

Similarly, in sentence 25a *oligarchy* is the object of *establishing*:

(25a)   Establishing an *oligarchy* is a common byproduct of the growth of organizations.

In sentence 25b, it's become a verb:

(25b)   *Oligarching* is a common byproduct of the growth of organizations.

As you pursue verbing, we have two words of caution. First, be sure that the new verb captures the meaning of the words it's replacing. For example, in our first attempts to write this section, we thought *gist* was a good candidate for verbing, as shown in the following pair of sentences:

(26a) Adults readily recall the *gist* of narratives.

(26b) Adults *gist* narratives.

In fact, *gist* didn't work well as a verb because *gist narratives* does not necessarily imply *recall the gist of narratives*. It might mean that adults readily perceive the gist of narratives or refer to other actions people might perform on *gist*.

Second, as was true for words created from prefixes and suffixes, verbed words are best used after the context establishes their meaning, such as at the end of an introduction or discussion section. And we recommend you create no more than one or two new words per paper. With one (or two) new words, readers are likely to enjoy the novelty and appreciate the descriptive power of the new word. With more than two new words, readers will find you guilty of way-over-the-top writing.

Exercise 3.9

Enliven these sentences by making the italicized word a verb.

1. Women in management positions often encounter a *glass ceiling*.
2. After adolescents commit a *crime* and get away with it, they decide that this activity is less risky.
3. People who violate economic *taboos* (e.g., they sell babies, they bribe) often try to make such actions seem less offensive by making them seem commonplace.
4.* Unions help to foster a sense of *community* among workers.

Wrap Up

1. Make your writing more concise by changing negatives to affirmatives, deleting what readers can infer, replacing phrases with words, and including only essential adjectives and adverbs.
2. Make your writing livelier by writing actively, relying on figures of speech (simile, metaphor, antimetabole), and creating new words.

For Practice

1. Search for negatives and replace with affirmatives, replace phrases with words, and decide which adjectives and adverbs are unnecessary.
2. In an introduction or discussion section, clarify a complex idea with a simile or metaphor.
3. In the last paragraph of a discussion, create a final sentence that includes antimetabole.
4. In an introduction or discussion section, create new words by adding a prefix or suffix, using hyperhyphenation, or verbing.

ANSWERS TO EXERCISES

Exercise 3.1

1. Our baseline model assumes that patterns of exchange mobility are stable over time.
2. Online social networks could reduce social segregation because adolescents could befriend agemates from other schools.
3. Moving allows residents to create a new narrative of safety, even when residents move nearby.

Exercise 3.2

1. The sample is representative, includes multiple indicators of race, and is large ~~in size~~.
2. Of the students who ~~completely~~ finished the academic secondary school track, 53% went to college.
3. Groups sometimes reach consensus ~~of opinion~~ based on the attitudes of one influential person.

Exercise 3.3

1. The evidence suggests that neither fertility nor mortality will change ~~in the near future~~ *soon*.
2. When people in blended families experience conflict, they ~~have a tendency~~ *tend* to blame it on tension related to their children.

3. Immigrants' proficiency in English is determined by several traits acquired ~~during the time~~ *while* they were growing up in their home countries.

Exercise 3.4

Adjectives and adverbs are in italics.

1. *Married* individuals who *verbally* report having a *truly happy* marriage *actually* have *better physical* health and *increased* longevity.

Individuals who have a *happy* marriage have *better physical* health and *increased* longevity.

2. *Social* class is a *meaningful* characteristic that *generally* influences *various* perceptions of confidence.

Social class is a characteristic that influences perceptions of confidence.

3. Children of *foreign* immigrants *typically* enter US schools with *somewhat limited* knowledge of US culture, yet they *often* are *relatively more successful* in school than their *native-born* peers.

Children of immigrants enter US schools with *limited* knowledge of US culture, yet they *often* are *more successful* in school than their *native-born* peers.

Exercise 3.5

1. In the United States, COVID-19 raced through African American communities like the anchor on a relay team.
2. Collective locomotion of the sort that occurs in street actions typically moves erratically, like a ship directed by an unskilled navigator.
3. Released prisoners often report feeling estranged and out of place in civilian life, like a violin in a marching band.

Exercise 3.6

1. Social movements are not innovative because they are successful, instead they are successful because they are innovative.
2. When elected officials lose sight of outcomes, the likely outcome of elections is that they will lose.
3. What matters most is not protecting the wages of workers who provide health care but, instead, protecting the health care of workers who lack wages.

Exercise 3.7

1. pseudotax
2. mistax
3. taxaholics

Exercise 3.8

1. The *perceive-the-social-system-as-fair* motive is particularly well established ...
2. The findings help to explain the prevalence of *offended-by-TV-news* evangelicals.
3. *Seeking-forever-home* families take their time to find homes that meet their ideal homes and neighborhoods.

Exercise 3.9[4]

1. Women in management positions often *glass ceiling*.
2. After adolescents *crime* and get away with it, they decide that this activity is less risky.
3. People who *taboo* economically (e.g., they sell babies, they bribe) often try to make such actions seem less offensive by making them seem commonplace.

Notes

1 One common adverb to avoid is *very* because *very* + *adjective* typically can be replaced with a single adjective that's more precise. For example, replace *very important* with *vital*, replace *very seldom* with *rare*, and replace *very large* with *enormous*.

2   Black Friday is the Friday after the American Thanksgiving holiday and marks the start of the Christmas shopping season in the United States. Stores are usually packed with shoppers looking for good deals.

3   This sentence illustrates one of the aforementioned obstacles: a cliché.

4   Yes, some of these sound strange on first reading. But, no doubt so did *google*, *impact*, *podium*, *dialog*, etc. when first used as verbs!

Lesson 4

The Art of Fine Paragraphs

Lesson Outline

- Structure
- Flow
- Length

If your sentences are clean, compelling, and lively, you're well on the way to joining the A-list of authors in sociology. But just as buying the best ingredients doesn't guarantee you'll prepare a gourmet meal, outstanding sentences alone won't guarantee an outstanding manuscript. You need to be able to assemble those excellent sentences into a coherent paragraph, a process we examine in this lesson. We'll start by examining the structure of paragraphs, then consider their flow and length.

Structure

A paragraph includes several sentences about one main idea. Not two main ideas, not three or four—just one. If you find yourself drifting to a new idea, start a new paragraph. That idea is normally expressed in the first sentence, called the topic sentence. Because it introduces the central idea of the paragraph, the topic sentence is crucial. It's followed by supporting sentences that develop the idea introduced in the topic sentence. A paragraph sometimes ends with a closing statement that restates the main idea and summarizes the supporting information.

The Topic Sentence

A strong topic sentence includes two parts: a topic and a controlling idea that specifies what the paragraph will say about the topic. In sentence 1,

DOI: 10.4324/9781003328285-4

for example, the topic is the Great Migration, and the controlling idea is that this increased racial segregation:

(1)   The Great Migration increased racial segregation in virtually all major cities in the Northeast and Midwest.

Thus, the topic sentence gives the reader a road map for the rest of the paragraph—it will focus on the impact of the Great Migration on racial segregation. Similarly, in sentence 2, the topic is American teenagers and young adults; the controlling idea is that they have high expectations for success:

(2)   Today, many American teenagers and young adults have high expectations for success.

Exercise 4.1

Identify the topics and controlling ideas in these sentences.

1. Resistance groups are more likely to revolt when they perceive threat to be immediate and lethal.
2. Historically, "ideal workers" were those who could devote full time to work without concern for other obligations (e.g., to family).
3. Latino immigrants often report discrimination based on the color of their skin.
4.* Corporations that experience financial strain more often violate laws against price fixing.

Well-written topic sentences are worth the effort because readers sometimes skim an article by reading only topic sentences. Consequently, topic sentences need to identify each step in the argument you develop, particularly in the introduction and discussion sections (there's more on this idea in Lessons 5 and 7).

Paragraph Development

A topic sentence is followed by three to six sentences that elaborate the controlling idea. In sociological writing, that elaboration usually takes one of three forms. One common format is to elaborate by providing supporting details. Sentence 2, for example, might by elaborated by describing a few examples illustrating teenagers' and young adults' high expectations:

(3) For example, most teenagers believe that they will attend a four-year college. In addition, they believe that they will work in a profession (e.g., be a doctor, lawyer). Finally, most young adults believe that they will earn enough money to meet all their needs and many of their wants.

Each of these sentences illustrates the high expectations held by teenagers and young adults.

In a second common format, the controlling idea involves competing theories, alternative hypotheses, or other kinds of contrasts. Sentence 4a illustrates a topic sentence for this sort of paragraph:

(4a) Parole officers serve two sometimes contradictory roles.

In the rest of the paragraph, the contrasting elements are described. With sentence 4a, this involves contrasting different roles for parole officers:

(4b) Parole officers serve two sometimes contradictory roles. On the one hand, parole officers are expected to devise treatment plans that will help to rehabilitate offenders. On the other hand, they are expected to provide surveillance that will protect the community from offenders who may dangerous.

This kind of paragraph is often crucial in developing arguments in a manuscript and consequently it's essential that it be written well. One formula for such a paragraph is to begin with a topic sentence that mentions alternative theories, hypotheses, explanations, or patterns of evidence. This is followed by *On the one hand* and a description of the first theory. Next comes *On the other hand* with a description of the second theory. Paragraph 5 illustrates this approach:

(5) Scholars have offered two competing explanations for the widespread support of democracy in authoritarian countries. *On the one hand*, people living in authoritarian countries may value democracy so much because they lack it. *On the other hand*, people living

in authoritarian countries may value democracy so much because their understanding of democracy often includes authoritarian notions but not liberal ones.

On one hand and *on the other hand* make a great tool for showing the readers the beginning and end of each description.[1]

The last common type of paragraph format describes processes that unfold over time. These paragraphs often describe sequences of behavior, historical change, or steps in an analysis. Paragraph 6 illustrates this structure:

(6)   To evaluate our hypotheses, Ordinary Least Squares (OLS) regression was used to assess the impact of volunteering on loneliness. First, we entered the widowhood variable into the model while controlling for demographic and personality variables. Next, we entered volunteer engagement behavior. Finally, we entered an interaction term between widowhood and volunteer behavior.

This paragraph describes the three steps in the analysis.

Exercise 4.2

Unscramble the sentences and then identify the type of development used in each paragraph.

1.   In addition, women are more likely to miss work when problems arise in childcare or when children are ill. Both men and women experience conflict between obligations to their job and to their family, but women are more likely to resolve these conflicts in favor of their family. Finally, women are more likely to shift to part-time work to reduce conflicts. Women put more limits on their work, such as not being willing to travel.

2.   A settlement of litigation against one establishment in an industry may encourage other establishments in that industry to change. Finally, political pressure can draw attention to issues of equity and encourage adherence to Equal employment opportunity (EEO) laws. EEO laws provide several ways to address discrimination in the workplace indirectly.

Additionally, firms that wish to obtain contracts with the federal government must comply with EEO laws.

3. Alternatively, couples might be similar in education and health because they use only education to select partners, but education is highly correlated with health. Married couples often are similar in many characteristics (e.g., education, race, health), a phenomenon that has been explained in two ways. Couples might be similar in education and health because they use both, independently, to select partners.

4.* Finally, in the 1980s and 1990s, coverage declined but was still greater than in the first half of the century. For the first half of the century, media coverage was scant. Media coverage of the African American Civil Rights movement changed over the 20th century. When protest events became more frequent during the 1950s, 1960s, and 1970s, coverage increased substantially.

Concluding Sentence

Most descriptions of paragraph structure include a concluding sentence that summarizes the paragraph's main points. However, for effective writing in sociology, these are more appropriate for some paragraphs than others. For a paragraph that lists supporting information, a concluding sentence might refer to each of the cited points. For example, the italicized sentence summarizes the paragraph from passage 3:

(7)   Today, many American teenagers and young adults have high expectations for success. For example, most teenagers believe that they will attend a four-year college. In addition, they believe that they will work in a profession (e.g., doctor, lawyer). Finally, most young adults believe that they will earn enough money to meet all their needs and many of their wants. *Thus, in terms of education, work, and income, American teenagers and young adults expect success.*

As in passage 7, concluding sentences are often marked by words that signal a conclusion, such as *thus*, *in summary*, or *to conclude*.

In paragraphs that contrast theories or hypotheses, a summary sentence should briefly cite each of the alternatives:

(8)   Parole officers serve two sometimes contradictory roles. On the one hand, parole officers are expected to devise treatment plans that will help to rehabilitate offenders. On the other hand, they are expected to provide surveillance that will protect the community from offenders who may be dangerous. *In summary, parole officers often deal with offenders in both therapeutic and policing roles.*

Notice that in this concluding sentence, the two alternatives are described in parallel structure.

For these two kinds of paragraphs (i.e., those providing supporting information and those contrasting alternatives), a concluding sentence is most useful when the paragraphs are relatively long. In this case, readers often benefit from a reminder of the controlling idea and the evidence supporting it. And a concluding sentence provides a good sense of closure when the paragraph is at the end of the introduction or discussion sections. But for paragraphs that include only three or four relatively simple sentences, concluding sentences are optional.

For the third common type of paragraph structure—those devoted to describing processes—concluding sentences are less common. This is particularly true for paragraphs describing research methods; concluding sentences are unnecessary. For paragraphs that describe behaviors or processes unfolding over time, a concluding sentence might simply list the first and last steps, perhaps with an illustrative intermediate step.

Exercise 4.3

Add a concluding sentence to each of the paragraphs in Exercise 4.2.

Flow

A well-defined structure is an essential element of an effective paragraph. However, just as important are two other features: a seamless transition from one sentence to the next and a common perspective across all sentences in the paragraph.

Sentence Transitions

Readers generally prefer paragraphs where sentences flow smoothly from one to the next, where ideas of the current sentence seem to emerge naturally from those expressed in prior sentences. To illustrate, compare passages 9a and 9b, in which the topic sentence is the same, but the second sentence differs.

(9a)   In a generalized exchange, a person gives something to another person without receiving something from that person in return. Helping a driver whose car won't start or helping a person who has fallen are examples of generalized exchange.

(9b)   In a generalized exchange, a person gives something to another person without receiving something from that person in return. Examples of generalized exchange include helping a driver whose car won't start or helping a person who has fallen.

Most readers find passage 9b is easier to read than passage 9a.

Similarly, compare passages 10a and 10b, which differ only in the second sentence.

(10a) People involved in religion—through personals beliefs or active participation in religious institutions—tend to have better mental health. Such people are less prone to depression and anxiety.

(10b) People involved in religion—through personals beliefs or active participation in religious institutions—tend to have better mental health. Depression and anxiety are less common in such individuals.

In this case, most readers believe that 10a is the easier passage; this passage seems to have better flow than passage 10b. Why? In passages 10a and 9b, the second sentence begins with information presented in the first sentence and then introduces new information. In passage 9b, the first sentence defines a generalized exchange. In the second sentence, the subject—*Examples of generalized exchange*—refers to the phenomenon mentioned in the first sentence. Then the new material—two examples of generalized exchange—appears, after its meaning has been well established. In contrast, in passage 9a, the second sentence begins with the examples, but their meaning isn't clear until the last five words of that sentence: *are examples of generalized exchange.*

This general principle—begin a sentence with familiar information and then introduce new information—explains why passage 10a is easier to read than passage 10b. In both passages, the first sentence establishes a link between mental health and people's involvement in religion. In passage 10a, the second sentence begins with the familiar idea (*Such people*) and then introduces specific domains in which they have better mental health. In contrast, the second sentence in passage 10b leads with new information about specific domains of mental health, and its significance isn't clear until the last half of the sentence.

Thus, starting sentences with familiar information establishes a context for new information and creates the sense of flow readers love. In other words, new ideas seem to appear seamlessly when they are firmly grounded in what the reader has read already. And there's an added benefit: leading with familiar information puts the new information at the end of the sentence, prime territory for the emphasis new information needs (as described on pages 21–28).

The familiar→new principle also explains why nominalizations and passive voice are valuable: each can be used to begin a sentence with familiar information.

(11)   Immigrants in detention centers are sometimes confined alone in a cell. Such solitary *confinement* is more common when detainees have mental illness or come from the Middle East.

In passage 11, *confinement* is a handy nominalization because it encapsulates the meaning of the first sentence and allows the second sentence to begin with familiar information.

Passive voice also allows you to start sentences with familiar information. In passage 12a, the second sentence begins with new information about tasks assigned to domestic workers:

(12a)   Worldwide nearly 70 million people—about 80% of them women—are employed as domestic workers. Preparing meals, caring for children, and cleaning houses are reasons why households hire domestic workers.

In contrast, in passage 12b, the second sentence relies on passive voice to lead with familiar information (*They* referring to *domestic workers*):

(12b)   Worldwide nearly 70 million people—about 80% of them women—are employed as domestic workers. They are hired to prepare meals, to care for children, and to clean houses.

Nominalizations and passive voice are useful to begin sentences with familiar information, but you shouldn't take that as an invitation to use them all the time. Nominalizations and passive voice are not recommended for good storytelling because they make it harder to identify characters and their actions. However, in this case, that loss is balanced by enhancing flow across sentences. (And this serves as a reminder that the recommendations we present here are rules of thumb that sometimes conflict.)

Exercise 4.4

Revise the second sentence in each passage to improve flow.

1. The New Deal spawned segregationist housing policy. Redlining, in which creditworthy applicants were denied loans solely based on the neighborhoods—typically African American—in which they lived, was one such policy.
2. In the Netherlands, children reared by same-sex parents have higher test scores than children reared by different-sex parents. Compensation theory, which states that same-sex parents invest more time and energy in child rearing, could explain this finding.
3. Adult children who care for aging parents often report much stress. The need to manage caregiving with other demanding roles, such as parenting their children, may be the source of this stress.
4.* Members of stigmatized groups often use strategies to create favorable impressions with other people. When other people seem to be stereotyping them, stigmatized individuals implement these strategies.

Finally, by design, some paragraphs have sentences that do not flow directly from one to the next. For example, when describing sequences of events, successive steps may have different contents, making it difficult to begin following sentences with familiar information. Passage 13a (a revised version of passage 6) illustrates this problem:

(13a) To evaluate our hypotheses, Ordinary Least Squares (OLS) regression was used to assess the impact of volunteering on loneliness. We entered the widowhood variable into the model while controlling for demographic and personality variables. We entered volunteer engagement behavior. We entered an interaction term between widowhood and volunteer behavior.

In this case, words that indicate sequence (e.g., *then*, *next*, *finally*, *first*, *second*, *third*) are useful to help the reader remember that successive sentences are linked only by order, not specific content. Passage 13b shows how the addition of these words alerts the reader to the organization of the paragraph.

(13b) To evaluate our hypotheses, Ordinary Least Squares (OLS) regression was used to assess the impact of volunteering on loneliness. *First*, we entered the widowhood variable into the model while controlling for demographic and personality variables. *Next*, we entered volunteer engagement behavior. *Finally*, we entered an interaction term between widowhood and volunteer behavior.

First, *next*, and *finally* provide the reader with explicit cues about the sequence of events and allow sequence to provide a sense of flow.

Exercise 4.5

Add transition words to help improve the flow of the paragraphs by making their organization more apparent.

1. For this qualitative study on the impact of internship experiences, we conducted in-depth interviews with college seniors. We asked academic advisors to identify departments where students routinely had internships. We invited seniors in those departments who had had internships to participate. We conducted an hour-long interview in which we asked participants about their internship experiences. We transcribed the interviews and coded them into themes and categories.
2. Racially based gangs in prisons simultaneously serve two important functions. They provide an organization that stabilizes prisons, protecting inmates who are members and intimidating those who are not. They control illicit economic activities within prisons, such as distributing drugs and arranging for prostitutes.

3.* Social movements, such as the American Civil Rights movement, typically develop through four stages. People experience widespread concerns and feelings of discontent that cause
movements to emerge; at this point, they lack organization.
Concerns become more clearly defined, strategies to address
them are developed, and protests are common. Movements
become organized formally and trained staff implement strategies. Movements decline because they succeed, are repressed,
or are co-opted into the mainstream.

A Common Perspective

Smooth transitions between sentences help to create a paragraph that
flows, but they aren't enough, as passage 14a shows:

(14a) The impact of immigration is often wide ranging. The arrival of
many immigrants raises concerns about their impact on wages
and employment for natives. In addition, immigration in an ethnically homogenous country increases that country's heterogeneity. Finally, the presence of many immigrants can change public
support for social policy, such as welfare spending.

In terms of structure, passage 14a begins with a topic sentence that
focuses on the impact of immigration, followed by three sentences that
illustrate common consequences of immigration. Although the structure is clear, passage 14a doesn't flow particularly well. Why? Passage
14b provides some clues. It has the same second and fourth sentences as
passage 14a, but the first and third sentences (in italics) differ.

(14b) *The impact of immigrants is often wide ranging.* The arrival of many
immigrants raises concerns about their impact on wages and
employment for natives. *In addition, in an ethnically homogenous
country, immigrants increase that country's heterogeneity.* Finally, the
presence of many immigrants can change public support for
social policy, such as welfare spending.

The difference is that each sentence in passage 14b adopts a common perspective or common viewpoint—each talks about immigration in terms
of the people involved: immigrants. In contrast, passage 14a alternates

between talking about immigration as an abstract concept (sentences 1 and 3) and immigration as an action that involves people (sentences 2 and 4). Alternating between these two perspectives (abstraction vs. people) disrupts the sense of flow.

Passages 15a and 15b show the same pattern.

(15a) People are not as lonely when they interact with others, but the most beneficial "others" depend on their culture. On the one hand, in individualist societies, friendship interactions help to reduce loneliness. On the other hand, people who live in collectivist societies benefit from interacting with families.

This brief paragraph doesn't flow well because it waffles between describing loneliness in terms of people's experiences (sentences 1 and 3) and as an abstraction (sentence 2). Passage 15b is better because it adopts a common viewpoint: sentence 2 has been changed so that it, like the others, describes grief in terms of people's experiences.

(15b) People are not as lonely when they interact with others, but the most beneficial "others" depend on their culture. On the one hand, people who live in individualist societies benefit from interacting with friends. On the other hand, people who live in collectivist societies benefit from interacting with families.

This passage flows because it consistently talks about people interacting with others. Thus, readers experience flow when the sentences in a paragraph share a common perspective in talking about the ideas from the topic sentence. To determine whether the sentences in a paragraph have a common viewpoint, compare the subjects of the sentences. When sentences share a common viewpoint, the sentences typically have similar subjects. For example, in passage 15b, the subject of each sentence is *people*.

Exercise 4.6

Edit the sentences so they have a common perspective.

1. Volunteering often contributes to successful aging. For example, volunteers report greater meaning in their lives. Moreover, volunteering may enhance older adults' cognitive functioning.

Lastly, volunteers sometimes experience improved physical health.

2. Eviction has many repercussions. Evicted families often experience considerable stress, in part because they often must find new housing with little notice. Eviction often leads to reduced income because eviction impairs work performance. Evicted families sometimes report declines in health because they move to substandard housing.

3.* Unemployment has consequences beyond the obvious loss of income. They typically report being less satisfied with life. This drop in life satisfaction is not completely offset by new employment.

Length

One part of developing your voice is creating paragraphs reasonably consistent in length. For the three types of paragraphs described on pages 54–56, four to seven sentences are usually adequate. For example, when elaborating a topic sentence by providing supporting evidence, a six-sentence paragraph might include four sentences that provide supporting information, plus topic and concluding sentences. The four sentences are usually enough to document the claims made in the topic sentence. More than four pieces of supporting information is often overkill: it makes the paragraph longer but doesn't make the argument more compelling (often because the additional evidence is weaker).

This length also works well for paragraphs contrasting alternative views or describing processes that unfold over time. For example, a six-sentence paragraph might include two sentences to describe each alternative, plus topic and concluding sentences. A seven-sentence paragraph could include three sentences for each alternative and a topic sentence, but no concluding sentence. In paragraphs describing processes, a six-sentence paragraph would include a topic sentence, plus descriptions of five steps. If there are more than five steps, it's probably best to create two groups of steps and devote a separate paragraph to each.

Exercise 4.7

Fix these paragraphs that are too long.

1. All landlords screen tenants but different types of landlords use different methods. On the one hand, professional landlords more often use formal techniques to determine a tenant's eligibility. That is, they evaluate tenants based on their income, credit score, and criminal history to decide whether a tenant is likely to pay rent reliably. On the other hand, amateur landlords typically rely on subjective "gut-based" evaluations to determine a tenant's eligibility. They evaluate tenants based on their appearance and behavior, their family status, and their responses to "home-made" questionnaires. Both methods can lead to racial discrimination in housing. The professional landlords' formal techniques often include measures (e.g., credit scores) that are racially biased. In addition, the amateur landlords' gut-based decisions often rely upon the extent to which prospective tenants defy racial stereotypes.

2. Street gangs facilitate violence in three distinct ways. First, gangs are often in conflict with rival gangs over status or reputation, conflict that often leads to violence. In fact, such intergroup conflict is so pervasive that some gangs take on names that mock their rivals (e.g., Deuce Killers). Second, gangs often engage in reciprocal acts of violence, such that one gang's act of violence leads to a rival's retaliatory act of violence. Reciprocating violence in this manner also serves to protect the gang. Third, gangs achieve status when they consistently win street battles. This sort of jockeying for status is common to other nonviolent groups that compete (e.g., Apple vs. Microsoft).

3.* Today, fixed work schedules are giving way to more flexible work arrangements, but the extent of this change depends on several factors. First, the characteristics of workers matter. Older and more educated workers report greater flexibility. In contrast, women report less flexibility. Second, the characteristics of jobs matter. Full-time workers report less flexibility. However, self-employed workers and those with higher earnings report greater flexibility. Third, characteristics of countries matter. Workers in countries with greater GDP and greater social welfare spending report greater flexibility. In addition, workers in countries where union membership is greater report flexibility.

Of course, some paragraphs will naturally be longer than others due to the complexity of the controlling idea. That said, avoid paragraphs substantially longer or shorter than your average paragraph. Amid a slew of 5- to 7-sentence paragraphs, 3- and 15-sentence paragraphs cause trouble. Readers usually find much-longer-than-average paragraphs to be dense, in part because the length causes them to lose track of the paragraph's structure. They find much-shorter-than-average paragraphs to be underdeveloped and wonder why you didn't have more to say on the topic.

Wrap Up

1. Make a paragraph's organization obvious by starting with a clear topic sentence and using the remaining sentences to flesh out the ideas in that topic sentence.
2. Make your writing flow by creating seamless transitions from one sentence to the next (always leading with familiar information) and by adopting a common perspective for all sentences in the paragraph.
3. Keep paragraphs relatively short (e.g., four to seven sentences) and avoid paragraphs substantially shorter or longer than your average paragraph.

For Practice

1. Read just the topic sentences in an Introduction. Do they convey the gist of the author's argument? If not, revise them so they do.
2. Find paragraphs that don't flow well, either because transitions across sentences are awkward or because the sentences don't have a common perspective. Revise for better flow.
3. Search for paragraphs in an introduction or discussion section that seem unusually short or long compared to the others. Do they seem out of place? Why?

ANSWERS TO EXERCISES

Exercise 4.1

1. Topic = Resistance groups; controlling idea = they revolt when they perceive immediate and lethal threats.
2. Topic = ideal workers; controlling idea = they devoted full time to work without concern for other obligations.
3. Topic = Latino immigrants; controlling idea = they report discrimination based on skin color.

Exercise 4.2

1. Both men and women experience conflict between obligations to their job and to their family, but women are more likely to resolve these conflicts in favor of their family. Women put more limits on their work, such as not being willing to travel. In addition, women are more likely to miss work when problems arise in childcare or when children are ill. Finally, women are more likely to shift to part-time work to reduce conflicts. [Structure = supporting details.]
2. Equal employment opportunity (EEO) laws provide several ways to address discrimination in the workplace indirectly. A settlement of litigation against one establishment in an industry may encourage other establishments in that industry to change. Additionally, firms that wish to obtain contracts with the federal government must comply with EEO laws. Finally, political pressure can draw attention to issues of equity and encourage adherence to EEO laws. [Structure = supporting details.]
3. Married couples often are similar in many characteristics (e.g., education, race, health), a phenomenon that has been explained in two ways. Couples might be similar in education and health because they use both, independently, to select partners. Alternatively, couples might be similar in education and health because they use only education to select partners, but education is highly correlated with health. [Structure = comparison.]

Exercise 4.3

1. Both men and women experience conflict between obligations to their job and to their family, but women are more likely to resolve these conflicts in favor of their family. Women put more limits on their work, such as not being willing to travel. In addition, women are more likely to miss work when problems arise in childcare or when children are ill. Finally, women are more likely to shift to part-time work to reduce conflicts. *Thus, to reduce-work family conflicts, women put limits on work, miss work, and more often work part-time.*

2. Equal employment opportunity (EEO) laws provide several ways to address discrimination in the workplace indirectly. A settlement of litigation against one establishment in an industry may encourage other establishments in that industry to change. Additionally, firms that wish to obtain contracts with the federal government must comply with EEO laws. Finally, political pressure can draw attention to issues of equity and encourage adherence to EEO laws. *In summary, EEO laws address discrimination by creating expectations within an industry, through constraints on federal contracts, and political pressure.*

3. Married couples often are similar in many characteristics (e.g., education, race, health), a phenomenon that has been explained in two ways. Couples might be similar in education and health because they use both, independently, to select partners. Alternatively, couples might be similar in education and health because they use only education to select partners, but education is highly correlated with health. *Thus, couples may resemble each other because they select based on many characteristics or because they select on one characteristic that is related to others.*

Exercise 4.4

1. The New Deal spawned segregationist housing policy. One such policy was redlining, in which creditworthy applicants were denied loans solely based on the neighborhoods—typically African American—in which they lived.

2. In the Netherlands, children reared by same-sex parents have higher test scores than children reared by different-sex

parents. This finding could be explained with the compensation theory, which states that same-sex parents invest more time and energy in child rearing.

3. Adult children who care for aging parents often report much stress. Such stress may stem from their need to manage caregiving with other demanding roles, such as parenting their children.

Exercise 4.5

1. For this qualitative study on the impact of internship experiences, we conducted in-depth interviews with college seniors. *First*, we asked academic advisors to identify departments where students routinely had internships. *Next*, we invited seniors in those departments who had had internships to participate. *Then*, we conducted an hour-long interview in which we asked participants about their internship experiences. *Finally*, we transcribed the interviews and coded them into themes and categories.

2. Racially based gangs in prisons simultaneously serve two important functions. They provide an organization that stabilizes prisons, protecting inmates who are members and intimidating those who are not. *At the same time*, they control illicit economic activities within prisons, such as distributing drugs and arranging for prostitutes.

Exercise 4.6

We've revised each paragraph two ways, once relying on constructs and once relying on people.

1. Volunteering often contributes to successful aging. For example, volunteering is associated with greater meaning in older adults' lives. Moreover, volunteering may enhance older adults' cognitive functioning. Lastly, volunteering is sometimes associated with improved physical health. OR

People who volunteer often age more successfully. For example, they report greater meaning in their lives. Moreover, older volunteers may have enhanced cognitive functioning. Lastly, they sometimes experience improved physical health.

2. Eviction has many repercussions. Eviction often produces considerable stress, in part because of the need to find new housing with little notice. Eviction often leads to reduced income because eviction impairs work performance. Eviction sometimes is linked to declines in health because the only available housing is substandard. OR

Families that are evicted endure many repercussions. They often experience considerable stress, in part because they often must find new housing with little notice. Evicted families often have less income because their performance at work suffers. They sometimes report declines in health because they move to substandard housing.

Exercise 4.7

1. This eight-sentence paragraph really has two parts. The first five sentences deal with the methods that landlords use to screen tenants. The last three sentences deal with the consequences of those methods for discrimination in housing. The fix is simple: split the one paragraph in two.

All landlords screen tenants but different types of landlords use different methods. On the one hand, professional landlords more often use formal techniques to determine a tenant's eligibility. That is, they evaluate tenants based on their income, credit score, and criminal history to decide whether a tenant is likely to pay rent reliably. On the other hand, amateur landlords typically rely on subjective "gut-based" evaluations to determine a tenant's eligibility. They evaluate tenants based on their appearance and behavior, their family status, and their responses to "home-made" questionnaires.

Both methods can lead to racial discrimination in housing. The professional landlords' formal techniques often include measures (e.g., credit scores) that are racially biased. In addition, the amateur landlords' gut-based decisions often rely upon the extent to which prospective tenants defy racial stereotypes.

2. This seven-sentence paragraph has a topic sentence followed by three pairs of sentences. The first sentence in each pair describes a way in which gangs facilitate violence. But the second sentence makes an offhand remark that doesn't bear centrally on the topic sentence. The simple fix is to drop the second sentence in each pair, leaving the topic sentence and one sentence to describe each of the three ways that gangs facilitate violence.

Street gangs facilitate violence in three distinct ways. First, gangs are often in conflict with rival gangs over status or reputation, conflict that often leads to violence. Second, gangs often engage in reciprocal acts of violence, such that one gang's act of violence leads to a rival's retaliatory act of violence. Third, gangs achieve status when they consistently win street battles.

Note

1   Never use *On the other hand* alone; always pair it with *On the one hand*. When you use *On the other hand* alone, many readers will assume they missed *On the one hand* and go back through the manuscript trying to find it.

Framing the Introduction

Lesson Outline

- Stating the problem (and hooking the reader!)
- Providing the rationale for your work
- Stating (or restating) the hypotheses and linking them to the design

You can use the tips we've described in Lessons 1–4 to improve all your writing, from emails to posts on social media to blog posts to op-eds! But beginning with this lesson, we want to take those tips a step further and show you how they can be used to write a clear and compelling report of your research. If you're an undergraduate, you might write such a report as a senior thesis; if you're a graduate student, you might write such a report as a doctoral dissertation. And, if you're a professional researcher, you might write such a report for publication in a journal. In all these cases, your report will begin with an introduction, where you will want to show your readers that the topic is timely and important, the approach is fresh and lively, and the methods are well-suited to the project.

We need to start with a note about language. We're using the term "introduction" to describe all material that appears prior to the "data and method" section in an article. This material can be structured in many ways. Because so many combinations are possible, we are not going to cover them all or tell you which one we think is "right." (To a large degree, the "right" one is a function of the aim of the report—senior thesis vs. manuscript for publication—and, for that matter, the journal where the report might be published.) Instead, we describe heuristics useful for a generic introduction that accomplishes three main aims: (1) it introduces the topic of your work and establishes why it's important; (2) it describes the theories and/or evidence on the topic that's relevant

DOI: 10.4324/9781003328285-5

to your work; and (3) it states the questions/hypotheses/expectations that drive your research.

Stating the Problem (and Hooking the Reader!)

The first part of the introduction—typically 1–3 paragraphs—is designed to introduce the topic of the study and pique the reader's curiosity. Too often research reports begin by describing the state of the research literature; sentence 1a illustrates this approach:

(1a) Sociologists have studied many features of racial identity but they have ignored the ways that biracial people select racial labels to describe themselves.

This approach makes your manuscript seem run-of-the-mill. A better strategy is to begin by talking about people, relationships, institutions, or policies. One way is to mention things that are familiar yet poorly understood.

(1b) People often complete forms in which they are asked to specify their race. Completing these forms can be challenging for biracial people because they are often forced to choose one race. Although this situation is common, we know little about how biracial people select labels to describe themselves.

Sentence 1b introduces the topic with an example familiar to all readers; the fact that we know little about such a familiar phenomenon is a good way to "hook" the reader.

Another effective strategy is to begin with a rhetorical question for the reader to ponder. Sentence 2a shows an unimaginative state-of-the-literature introductory sentence:

(2a) In a review of the literature on the influence of culture on parenting practices, Jones et al. (2015*) concluded that culture is a structure that encourages certain parenting choices and limits others, but that, in any given situation, parents choose from a variety of culturally sanctioned options.

* The study cited here is not real; we created the name and date explicitly for this example. In the remainder of this book, such made-up citations are identified by an asterisk after the date. Because these studies are not real, they do not appear in the reference list.

Sentence 2b is a variant that begins with a rhetorical question:

(2b)   Suppose your young child accidently broke a prized family heir-
       loom. Would you send them to their room as punishment or
       would you explain to them why they should be more careful next
       time? Research on the influence of culture on parenting choices
       suggests you have a variety of culturally appropriate parenting
       decisions you could make, but there is little evidence regarding
       how you would select between competing alternatives (Jones
       et al., 2015*).

A third useful strategy is to start with an interesting statistic. Sentence
3a introduces the topic in a straightforward but uninspired manner:

(3a)   Research on racial variation in adolescents' friendships has been
       conducted primarily in schools where most students are White.
       This is problematic because most Black and Hispanic students
       attend high schools where most students are non-White (Irwin
       et al., 2021).

In contrast, sentence 3b starts with a statistic that establishes a striking
imbalance between the kinds of schools featured in research on ado-
lescent friendships and the schools that Black and Hispanic students
attend:

(3b)   Approximately 90% of the published articles on adolescents'
       friendships report research conducted in schools where at least
       60% of the students are White. This is problematic for research
       on racial variation in friendships because most Black and
       Hispanic students attend schools in which White students are in
       the minority (Irwin et al., 2021).

A fourth strategy is to begin with a case study or anecdote—a brief
description of a person (or persons) or an event that illustrates the
phenomenon of interest. Sentence 4a is a typical uninspired opening
sentence.

(4a) According to Kearl (2018), nearly one-third of all women report experiencing sexual harassment at their place of work.

In contrast, passage 4b starts with an anecdote that brings experience of sexual harassment at work to life:

(4b) In 2017, more than 80 women—including Angelina Jolie, Mira Sorvino, and Gwyneth Paltrow—came forward to accuse movie producer and studio head Harvey Weinstein of sexual assault. Weinstein's trial was front page news and resulted in a conviction and a 23-year prison sentence. His victims' experiences are far too common: nearly a third of all women report experiencing sexual harassment at their place of work (Kearl, 2018).

A fifth strategy is to start with a quotation from your data that both strikes at the heart of your paper and captures the reader's attention. Sentence 5a is a drab opening sentence.

(5a) Scholarly research has only begun to study the degree to which congregations are open to homosexuality (Putnam & Campbell 2010*), and even less is known about the experiences of homosexual men and women who grew up in the church.

In contrast, Sentence 5b opens with a quotation that both draws the reader into the respondent's individual story and establishes the main theme of the paper.

(5b) "I grew up in the church. I loved the church. I studied to be a pastor. I worked as an associate pastor. But when the leaders rejected the One Church Plan and voted in favor of the Traditional Plan, I had to leave. I was devastated. I felt betrayed. I let the church into my heart, and they rejected me because I'm a man who just happens to love another man." This man's experience suggests that some congregations are not open to homosexuality, but in fact little is known about the ways in which homosexual men and women who grew up in the church attempt reconcile the tensions between their sexual identity and their religious identity.

These approaches often engage a reader because they deal with social life, social change, or the social implications of human behavior—which is the focus of sociological research.

Exercise 5.1

Improve these introductory sentences by adding an example, a rhetorical question, an eye-popping statistic, or gripping anecdote.

1. Research on identity and work suggests that most people derive a sizable portion of their identity from their paid employment. However, it is unclear whether this has changed because of the COVID-19 pandemic.
2. Many Millennials are at risk of not having enough money in retirement and it is unclear whether Social Security will remain financially solvent when they begin retiring in 2043. In this study, we assessed five different interventions to assess which are most likely to increase Millennials' retirement saving behavior.
3. Research has clearly demonstrated that social class replication is likely to occur within families and across generations. However, it is unclear how often people between the ages of 20 and 30 who work in professional occupations secure their employment through an acquaintance of a family member and whether this is more common in middle-class families.
4. Many studies have evaluated why symptoms of depression differ significantly by race and gender.

Providing the Rationale for Your Work

This section of the introduction is sometimes known as the literature review, background, or theoretical framework. Regardless of the specific term, this section generally has a precise aim: to develop the rationale for your work, typically through a series of steps in which you identify what's known as well as what remains unknown or what is controversial. Depending on the type of research you are doing (and, to some degree, the aim of your report), you may focus on empirical evidence, you may focus on expectations for how processes should operate according to theory or for laying the groundwork for theory building. Some of the most compelling manuscripts combine both evidence and theory. Of course, in describing the rationale, you will refer to relevant evidence and prior theory, but the aim is specific: to document—with research findings and existing theory—the claims you make in the rationale for your study.

Regardless of the kind of research you're reporting, a good way to begin writing this section of the introduction is to briefly outline each step of your argument. For example, passage 6a includes four steps that provide the rationale for a study about whether living in the US South plays an important role in the lower rates of college enrollment observed among transgender high school students.

(6a)

a. There are more transgender high school students than before.
b. College enrollment is lower among transgender students.
c. Transgender students are also more likely to live in the South. High school students in the South are less likely to enroll in college.
d. Unclear whether region mediates the association between transgender identity and college enrollment.

Next, using the guidelines described in Lesson 4, translate each of these ideas into a topic sentence:

(6b)

a. In the US, high school students are increasingly likely to identify as transgender.
b. Transgender students are less likely than their cisgender peers to enroll in college.
c. Transgender students are also more likely to live in the South, relative to other regions, and high school students in the South are less likely to enroll in college than students in other regions.
d. Thus, one possible explanation for the enrollment gap between trans- and cis-gender high school students is that transgender students are more likely to live in a region of the US where college enrollment is less common; however, there is no evidence to support this explanation due to lack of population level data on high school students' gender identity.

The next step is to flesh out the claim made in each of these topic sentences, in a paragraph or two. For example, sentence c in passage 6b would be followed by sentences describing how both regional distribution of transgender students and regional variation influence college enrollment.

Exercise 5.2

Find an article and "reverse outline" the basic argument developed in the introduction. In other words, list the steps in the authors' argument that were used (or should have been used) to generate the topic sentences.

As you develop these paragraphs, it's essential that you follow some basic guidelines.

Put Issues, Ideas, and Findings in the Foreground and Studies and Scientists in the Background

Your rationale will be most effective if you frame it in terms of the issues at stake and not the studies in the literature (or the scientists who conducted the studies). Said differently, in reviewing the literature, you need to establish what's known and what isn't; that description should be fact or theory oriented, not study oriented. Focus on the evidence or theory, not the people who reported the evidence or developed the theory. Passage 7a, for example, illustrates a study-oriented description of a literature.

(7a)   There is an extensive literature on the role of power resources and institutions on differences between states in economic inequality. For example, Morella (1992*) showed that poverty rates were greater in states with lower levels of union participation. Maddon (2005*) provided evidence that median income was greater in states with more Democratic legislators. In contrast, Darvy (2010*) reported that the extent to which a state's legislature was comprised of members who were business owners or CEOs was inversely correlated with the state's minimum wage. Finally, Le (2009*) found that the percentage of judges on state courts of last resort appointed by Republican governors was associated with laws prohibiting union membership as a condition of employment.

The paragraph cites four studies, but it's difficult reading and puts the burden of interpreting these findings on the reader. In contrast, passage

7b is an outcome-oriented version of the passage where the text summarizes the state of the literature, citing relevant studies.

(7b)   There is an extensive literature on the role of power resources and institutions on differences between states in economic inequality. Unions and Democratic leaders are associated with reductions in poverty and larger median incomes (Maddon, 2005*; Morella, 1992*). In contrast, business-oriented legislatures and Republican-appointed judges are associated with lower minimum wage and laws prohibiting union membership as a condition of employment (Darvy, 2010*; Le, 2009*).

And by applying some of the tips from previous lessons, we might summarize everything in a single sentence:

(7c)   Power resources and institutions have important implications for differences between states in economic inequality: Unions and Democratic leaders are associated with less inequality whereas business-oriented legislatures and Republican-appointed judges are associated with increased inequality (Darvy, 2010*; Le, 2009*; Maddon, 2005*; Morella, 1992*).

Of course, it's common for the rationale you develop in an introduction to hinge on a critical study or two. You'll often need to describe these in greater detail, often by name. But this sort of description should be the exception; when using the literature to document the claims and theory in your rationale, put the studies in the background and emphasize the relevant findings.

Exercise 5.3

Revise these paragraphs to put the findings in the foreground.

1.   Many people in the US develop their identities in relation to paid employment. Joyce (2007*) reported that most people in the US derive a significant portion of their identity from paid work. However, Chin (2009*) showed that older women without career employment were more likely to develop identity from their husband's employment. Finally, Kim (1987*) found that non-Whites were generally less likely than Whites

to derive a significant portion of their identity from paid employment.

2. Research has revealed several factors that influence whether gentrification impacts the health of legacy residents (i.e., people who lived in the neighborhood before it began gentrifying). Bachman and Webster (2012*) reported that, for legacy residents who leave a gentrifying neighborhood, moving is associated with increased stress. Kahn and Aitken (2014*) found that legacy residents experience reduced social support after moving from a gentrifying neighborhood. In a study by McGrail et al. (2017*), legacy residents who remained in their neighborhood were able to increase physical activity through access to more green spaces, safer walking environments, and public outdoor exercise facilities. Finally, Alvarado (2016*) observed that, among legacy residents who remained in their neighborhood, increased rents and property taxes decreased residents' ability to purchase healthy food and get medical treatments.

3.* Over the past few decades, there has been a growing focus on the health implications of interracial marriage. O'byrne (2009*) found that individuals in interracial marriages report lower levels of self-reported health than people in same race marriages. Similarly, Browne (2011*) documented that, compared to people in same race marriages, people in interracial marriages experience a greater number of symptoms of depression. However, Mailor (2012*) reported that the association between interracial marriage and self-reported health depends on the racial composition of the interracial marriage. Moreover, McFadden (2014*) reported that the association between interracial marriage and symptoms of depression depends on a person's gender.

Be Fair in Describing the Literature

When you describe previous research that provides the background to your work, be sure to provide a complete and unbiased account. Incomplete or biased descriptions of relevant research usually annoy readers. In other words, readers will generally notice if your review omits work that isn't favorable to the arguments you develop.

In describing work it's essential that you're fair. For example, it's fine to identify shortcomings in prior work but be objective in your criticisms. And never engage in ad hominem arguments (where you attack the person doing the work, not the work itself). An effective rationale for research touches on all the necessary points, briefly, and in a manner that leaves people on all sides of an issue reasonably satisfied that the work has been presented accurately.

Cite Previous Work Selectively

As you draw upon the literature to frame your arguments, you may be tempted to cite all (or most) relevant studies. Don't! Exhaustively citing the literature has three problems. First, the aim of this part of your paper is not to describe the literature per se (as you would in a review paper) but to establish the logical, empirical, and theoretical bases for the arguments motivating your study. For this purpose, you simply need to show that each of your arguments is backed by evidence and/ or theory; you needn't cite all the supporting evidence. Said differently, the argument isn't necessarily more convincing if you cite five studies instead of just one or two. Second, many journals limit the number of pages or the number of references, a practice that forces you to be selective. Third, the standard practice of citing work by author and date of publication adds information to a sentence that interferes with the reader's comprehension of your text. For example, sentence 8a is easier to read (and much shorter) than sentence 8b.

(8a)   Early childhood advantage is associated with a wide array of beneficial outcomes in adulthood: children who grew up with more books in their houses are more likely to graduate from college, and adults whose parents were more educated and had higher occupational status have significantly greater incomes.

(8b)   Early childhood advantages is associated with a wide array of beneficial outcomes in adulthood (Santos et al., 2003*; Pignatti and Berthelot, 2002*, 2020*): children who grew up with more books in their houses are more likely to graduate from college (Bray et al., 2019*; Carrillo et al., 2012*; Cochran et al., 2005*) and adults whose parents were more educated and had higher occupational status have significantly greater incomes (Barr et al., 2018*; Drake et al., 2005*; Marquez et al., 2013*).

A general rule is that two citations should be adequate to bolster each step in your argument; more are overkill. When selecting studies to cite, one good choice is a recent review article that summarizes the relevant evidence. If a recent review is not available, you could cite an older review along with a recent study showing the same outcome. Feel free to cite your own work but only if it provides direct evidence and if it's the best evidence. Reviewers typically are critical of gratuitous self-citations.

Because citations are not part of the argument per se, we recommend putting them at the end of a sentence instead of scattering them throughout the sentence, as was done in sentence 9a.

(9a) Some factors that influence the restrictiveness of state abortion laws include the presence of prochoice advocacy groups (Mcknight et al., 1992*), female legislators (Pierce et al., 2004*), and the proportion of adults in a state who identify as Catholic (Villa et al., 2013*).

The first two citations in sentence 9a are hurdles: readers must jump them and find where the text resumes. In contrast, by placing the citations at the end, as in sentence 9b, the reader's path to understanding your sentence is uninterrupted by citations.

(9b) Some factors that influence the restrictiveness of state abortion laws include the presence of prochoice advocacy groups, female legislators, and the proportion of adults in a state who identify as Catholic (Mcknight et al., 1992*; Pierce et al., 2004*; Villa et al., 2013*).

This practice does move the supporting evidence a few words from the relevant text, but readers who are really invested in the topic can make the links. The remaining readers don't really care and are grateful that you've made the text easier to read. Of course, if the aim of the sentence is to contrast two views or hypotheses, you should separate those citations because they support different claims.

Many fledgling writers are nervous about citing research selectively; they fear doing so will antagonize individuals who review their manuscripts. In other words, novice scientists often worry that if they neglect to cite Willaims (2013*) and Willaims happens to review their manuscript, they will recommend the manuscript be rejected. In our experience, you needn't worry about this. As mentioned earlier, reviewers object strongly to a biased presentation of the literature, but they don't respond harshly to the absence of individual studies per se. They may suggest you cite additional studies. If the editor endorses that suggestion, go ahead and include the suggested studies. (And since your original manuscript has relatively few citations, adding two to three more won't be a problem.)

Similarly, some writers feel like they need to cite countless articles to prove how much they know about a topic when writing their introduction. Don't let yourself fall into this trap! While it may make you feel good to show your vast knowledge, it is generally a disservice to your manuscript. You need not cover all aspects, tangents, and variants of things related to your topic. Stay focused on claims that are necessary for your argument.

Stating (or Restating) the Hypotheses and Linking Them to the Design

The last paragraph (or two) of the introduction has a special role—you state your research questions, hypotheses, predictions, or expectations. You will frequently have stated these earlier in the manuscript in one form or another already; this paragraph simply reminds the reader of them so they are fresh in the reader's mind before they begin reading the data and method section.

Let's return to the study outlined on page 78 designed to determine whether living in the US South plays an important role in the lower rates of college enrollment observed among transgender high school students. The paragraphs leading up to the final paragraph have established that (1) transgender high school students are less likely to enroll in college, (2) that college enrollment is lower in the US South, and (3) transgender high school students are more likely to live in the US South. The paragraphs also claim that no studies have assessed whether living in the US South explains the lower rates of college enrollment among transgender high school students. Thus, the objective of this final paragraph is to remind the reader of the aim of the work and develop related hypotheses. Passage 10 illustrates one possibility:

(10)   The aim of the present work was to determine whether living in the US South plays an important role in the lower rates of college enrollment observed among transgender high school students. Based on the aforementioned evidence, we developed the following hypothesis: H_1 *When the region where students live is controlled statistically, transgender and cisgender students will no longer differ in college enrollment.*

Notice that passage 10 begins by stating the aims of the study and ends with a statement of the expected pattern of results. One common mistake in writing this paragraph is to use present or future tense. In fact, you're describing events that have already occurred, so the past tense is appropriate.

To end this lesson, we remind you that the introduction is one of the most important sections in the manuscript. If your introduction is really well written, readers will be so excited at the end of this section that they'll jump directly to the results to see if the study worked out as you expected.

Exercise 5.4

Create an introduction-ending paragraph from the information provided.

1. Do racial differences in gender stereotypes reduce Asian men's chances of securing collegiate coaching jobs?
    Outline:
    a) There is an increase of Asian men in collegiate and professional athletics.
    b) Despite this increase, there are still significantly fewer Asian division 1 collegiate coaches.
    c) Asians (regardless of gender) are viewed as more feminine that Whites or Blacks.
    d) There is no evidence of whether accounting for racial differences in gender stereotypes plays a significant role in why Asian men are underrepresented as college coaches.
2. Has the pace at which women have made inroads into occupations traditionally held by men slowed for both college-educated and non-college-educated women?
    Outline:
    a) Since the 1990s, more women complete college than men.
    b) There is an increasing gap between women's and men's college completion.
    c) At the same time, the pace at which women have made inroads into occupations traditionally held by men has been reduced by half.
    d) However, it is unclear whether the pace at which women have made inroads into occupations traditionally held by

men has slowed for both college-educated and non-college-educated women.

3.* Does age discrimination in employment explain much of the poverty gap between older unmarried Whites and older unmarried non-Whites?

   a) Twenty percent of all unmarried people over 65 live in poverty.

   b) However, compared to older unmarried non-Hispanic Whites, the poverty rate is about twice as large for unmarried Blacks and unmarried Asians, and two and a half times larger for unmarried Hispanics.

   c) Although all older people face potential age discrimination in employment, it is more common for non-Whites.

   d) It is unclear, however, how big a role age discrimination in employment plays in the increased chances of poverty for non-White unmarried people over 65.

Wrap Up

1. Use a good example, rhetorical question, surprising fact, anecdote, or quotation from your data to hook the reader into reading your paper.

2. As you structure the argument that motives your work, put the theory and evidence in the foreground (and the studies yielding the evidence in the background), present the evidence accurately, and cite evidence selectively.

3. In the last paragraph (or two) of the introduction, remind the reader of the main goals of the study and describe the hypotheses.

For Practice

1. Read the first paragraph or two of several articles. Do they begin with effective hooks? If so, what makes the hook effective? If not, rewrite them so they are more likely to grab the reader.

2. Find paragraphs that are study oriented; rewrite them to be outcome oriented.

3. Read the final paragraph(s) of the introduction from several articles; decide whether they provide a clear description of hypotheses and how those hypotheses are to be evaluated in the study.

Exercise 5.1

1. "What do you do?" is one of the most common questions people ask each other upon meeting, and most people in the US answer that question by sharing what they do for paid work. Indeed, research on identity and work suggest that most people derive a sizable portion of their identity from their paid employment. However, it is unclear whether this has changed because of the COVID-19 pandemic.

2. Currently, two-thirds of all Millennials have no money saved for retirement and no plans to begin saving. This is problematic because when they begin to retire in 2043, Social Security may not be financially solvent. Consequently, encouraging Millennials to save for retirement is essential and, in this study, we assessed five different interventions to achieve that aim.

3. "It was great! When I couldn't find an accounting job, my mom called one of her yoga friends and this friend got me a staff position at CIN" (*Ben Joyner, 39-year-old Certified Public Accountant*). Ben's experience is not uncommon: many professional workers find employment by researching out through a parent's network. However, it is unclear (a) whether there are social class differences in use of parental networks to secure employment and (b) how such differences could contribute to social class replication.

Exercise 5.3

1. Although most people in the US derive a significant portion of the identity from paid work (Joyce, 2007*), older women without career employment are more likely to develop identity from their husband's employment (Chin, 2009*), and non-Whites are generally less likely than Whites to derive a significant portion of their identity from paid employment (Kim, 1987*).

2. Research has revealed several factors that influence whether gentrification impacts the health of legacy residents (i.e., people who lived in the neighborhood before it began

gentrifying). Among legacy residents who leave a gentrifying neighborhood, moving is associated with increased stress and reduced social support (Bachman & Webster, 2012*; Kahn & Aitken, 2014*). Among legacy residents who remained in their neighborhood, physical activity increased through access to more green spaces, safer walking environments, and public outdoor exercise facilities (McGrail et al., 2017*), but increased rents and property taxes decreased residents' ability to purchase healthy food and get medical treatments (Alvarado, 2016*).

Exercise 5.4

1. The goal of this research was to assess whether racial differences in gender stereotypes reduce Asian men's chances of securing collegiate coaching jobs. Because Asian men are viewed as more feminine than Whites or Blacks, we hypothesized that athletic directors' gender stereotypes about Asian men will account for significant portions of why Asian men are not considered for many college coaching jobs.

2. The purpose of this study was to evaluate whether the pace at which women have made inroads into occupations traditionally held by men slowed for both college and non-college-educated women. Because women are increasingly more college educated than men, we hypothesized that the pace at which women have made inroads into occupations traditionally held by men slowed for non-college-educated women, but not for college-educated women.

Lesson 6

Reporting Results

Lesson Outline

- Getting started
- Describing the findings
- Assembling the pieces

Good movies and good novels always build to an exciting climax, the emotional highpoint of the story. For research reports, the results section is the climax of your story; in the introduction, you've set the stage, but the results section is where you tell readers what you've discovered; this is the exciting part of your paper.

As you write this section, stick to tell the storytelling approach we've emphasized throughout this book and that you used to write the introduction. Tell the reader what happened and use the results to support your account. Keep the results in the foreground and the data and analyses in the background. In other words, the data and methods are to the results section what citations are to the introduction and discussion sections—they document the story but aren't the story itself.

Getting Started

You probably have a stack of memos and quotes, or a pile of descriptive data and analyses. Avoid the temptation to start writing by summarizing them, one by one. That approach highlights the data and analyses themselves instead of the key themes or findings. A better approach to good storytelling of results is to think of this section as a photo essay. Books in this genre include evocative photographs surrounded by a modest amount of explanatory text. Applied to the results section, this means you'll include a few quotes, tables, and/or figures that depict the important themes and findings. You'll also provide text that walks the

DOI: 10.4324/9781003328285-6

reader through the major themes and findings and provides the necessary qualitative and/or quantitative method documentation as support.

The first step is to pick the evocative photos. Of course, these typically won't be actual photos but instead will be subheadings, tables, and/or figures. These should portray the essential themes and findings—those you'd be eager to share with others so they can see why you're so excited.

For qualitative results, although you may have pictures, tables, or figures (the latter can be a great way to concisely summarize the main points of your argument), the figurative pictures you select for your photo essay come in the form of the subheadings you select for your results. These subheadings should reflect the central themes and main findings of your report.

With well-selected subheadings, the reader should be able to get the gist of your argument(s) just by skimming them. For instance, imagine your data included the following quote: "[M]edia tends to focus around queer tragedy ... but another real thing is being queer and happy. Like, that is normal ... Being happy is not in spite of being queer. It is a part of it" (Kaysen Ford; pulled from June 25, 2021 *Morning Edition*).

The subheading shown in 1a is an example of a subheading that fails to capture the main point of an argument or main themes from the quote above:

(1a)   *Media and Queer Identities*

Although this subheading does foreshadow the quote (and presumably the main findings drawn from an analysis of similar quotes), it fails to convey any substantive meaning, let alone key findings or themes. Compared to 1a, the subheading in 1b gives the reader a clear sense of a theme or key finding:

(1b)   *Despite Media Representations, Being Queer and Happy Is Normal.*

This subheading does a much better job of painting a picture of one of the main thematic findings from the results: for many queer people, being happy is more normal than feeling tragic.

By using an explicit heading like the one in 1b, some writers are concerned that people won't read through the actual written results. But, frankly, many people don't read articles linearly, and may not read all the results or quotes anyway. Given that, what seems better: (a) people don't read the quotes and walk away without a sense of the main themes, or (b) people only read the subheadings and walk away with a clear sense of the main themes? Despite the obvious false dichotomy here, we believe the latter is better. And although we encourage the storytelling approach, we discourage writing the results like a mystery novel—testing readers to see if they can guess what happens or figure it out before the end. It's better to lead with the lede and tell the reader what the story is about upfront.

Exercise 6.1

Look over the pairs of subheadings below. Explain why each one is either a descriptive placeholder or a concise statement of the theme or main findings. Which do you prefer and why?

1a.* Women's Education and Job Attainment.
1b.* Highly Educated Women Are Viewed as Overqualified.
2a. Why Are Asian American Women More Active in Social Justice Rallies?
2b. Gender Difference in Asian Americans' Participation in Social Justice Rallies.
3a. Making Sense of Growing Up with a Depressed Parent.
3b. Growing Up with a Depressed Parent Shapes Adults' Health, Job Security, and Marital Satisfaction.

For quantitative results, reports will often include graphs or tables. Some writers believe the choice of a graph or table is simply personal preference (or whether an author has access to fancy graphing software); that's not true. Graphs are generally better than tables, particularly when the pattern of results is important. Most readers can detect patterns much more quickly in a graph than a table. For example, Figure 6.1 and Table 6.1 show the same numbers, but the pattern—the dependent variable increases more rapidly among Group A than in Group B—leaps out of the figure but not the table.

Tables are generally preferred in two circumstances. The first is to provide descriptive statistics for an entire sample or by groups; Table 6.2 is an example. This is generally done to either illustrate how well the people in your study reflect the broader population they are intended to represent, or to evaluate differences across groups. In the latter instance, it's generally better to include both the means/proportions by group and the indicators of bivariate difference tests (usually with asterisks).

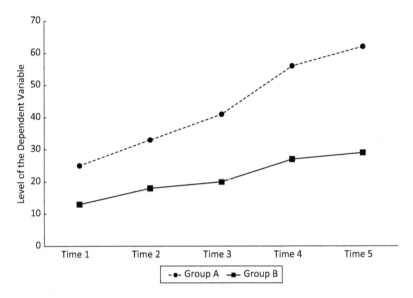

Figure 6.1 Change in the dependent variable over time, separately for Groups A and B.

Table 6.1 Changes over Time in the Dependent Variable, Separately for Groups A and B

Group	Independent Variable				
	Time 1	Time 2	Time 3	Time 4	Time 5
A	25	33	41	56	62
B	13	18	20	27	29

A second circumstance is when the reader needs to know exact values of variables instead of patterns. It is often easier for readers to interpret a well-crafted graph or figure derived from regression analyses than it is to interpret tabulated results (particularly regarding interactions terms or exponential terms). Nevertheless, it remains a common practice to provide a table showing the results of multiple regression analyses, where readers are interested in the specific values of regression coefficients; Table 6.3 is an example. Of course, you could always include both: use a graph or figure in the results section proper and refer to

Table 6.2 Means/Proportions and Bivariate Differences by Race/Ethnicity

	Overall	White	Black	Hispanic
All Votes Count	0.66	0.63***	0.87	0.71
Education				
– College	0.57	0.61***	0.46	0.46
– Some College	0.29	0.28***	0.34	0.33
– H.S.	0.14	0.12***	0.20	0.21
Race/Ethnicity				
– White	0.75	1.00***	0.00	0.00
– Black	0.08	0.00***	1.00	0.00
– Hispanic	0.17	0.00***	0.00	1.00
Age	53.50	55.83***	50.92	44.41
Gender				
– Man	0.45	0.47***	0.32	0.42
– Woman	0.55	0.53***	0.68	0.57
– Other	0.01	0.00***	0.01	0.01
	n = 10,752	n = 8,059	n = 884	n = 1,809

$^*p < .05$, $^{**}p < .01$, $^{***}p < .001$; significance indicates means/proportions are different by race according to a chi-square test for categorical variables and an ANOVA for continuous variables.

Table 6.3 Multiple Logistic Regression Analysis Predicting Confidence That All Mail-In and Absentee Ballots Were Counted in the 2020 Election

	b/se
Some College[a]	−0.857***
	(0.048)
H.S.[a]	−1.033***
	(0.063)
Black[b]	1.387***
	(0.104)
Hispanic[b]	0.482***
	(0.061)
Age	0.003*
	(0.001)
Women[c]	0.138**
	(0.043)
Other[c]	0.671*
	(0.337)
Intercept	0.558***
	(0.087)
AIC	12977.012

*p < .05., **p < .01, ***p < .01 (N = 10,752; coefficients are logit coefficients; reference categories are a = College, b = White, and c = Men)

the full regression table that you've provided in an appendix or online supplement.

Having decided which format will work best for your results, create a working version of a graph or table. Just a rough version will do for now; you can tweak it later.

Exercise 6.2

Decide whether these results are best suited for a graph and table and then construct that graph or table.

1. A longitudinal dataset was used to track racial differences in changes in cognition at three points (ages 60, 65, and 70) over 15 years. At each point, respondents completed a series of assessments from which an "overall cognition" score was calculated. Regression analyses were done, from which predicted values were calculated, For Blacks, the predicted values were 17.29, 16.32, and 15.38 (at ages 60, 65, and 70); for Hispanics, the predicted values were 18.24, 17.22, and 16.25; and for Whites the predicted values were 22.11, 21.31, and 19.49.

2. Survey data were used to assess factors that shape the percentage of a respondent's social network that is composed of friends (relative to family). For men, being married was associated with a 30% decrease in the percentage of network that is composed of friends, but no other factors in the model were associated with how much of the social network is friends for men. In contrast, for women being married was only associated with a 20% reduction in the percentage of network that is composed of friends, but not working was associated with an additional 15% reduction in percentage of network that is composed of friends. No additional factors in the model were associated with how much of the social network is friends for men.

Describing the Findings

With the subheadings, graphs, figures, and/or tables selected, it's time for the text that will "walk the reader" through your results. As we mentioned earlier, the best way to guide your readers is to tell a story, providing quotes and citing the analyses as necessary to support what you have to say. At this point, focus on the text supporting each sub-heading, figure, or table individually. Don't worry about weaving everything together to form a coherent results section; that comes later.

In the next few pages we focus on ethnographic results and multiple regression results to illustrate general techniques and principles of the storytelling approach to writing results with two common kinds of findings. So, while reading the following sections, keep in mind that (a) these are general suggestions, and (b) they may need to be modified for your specific methodological approach.

Findings from Ethnographic Research

In ethnographic research, writers often believe you should highlight as many of the interesting and compelling quotes as you can. However, this approach often lends itself to two sticking points. The first is that, given the limited space provided in journals, highlighting many interesting quotes frequently comes at the cost of providing clear and concise themes and findings for the reader.

The second sticking point is that if you just provide a slew of quotes—or even a combination of descriptions, quotes, and how you analyzed them—you put the burden of deriving meaning and extracting main findings or themes onto the reader. But it's your job as the writer to make those themes and main findings crystal clear. Presenting the quotes and describing the setting doesn't do that. It is your narrative about the data and analyses (along with well-selected subheadings) that makes the themes and findings clear. In other words, the data are collected and analyzed, but this should mostly be in the background of a results section; the findings (often the themes or main points derived from the analyses) should be at the foreground. Thus, the quotes you use should bolster your main narrative rather than highlight the data themselves.

A good rule of thumb is that for each point you are trying to make, one or two quotes should suffice. This gives you more space to write about what you found during your analyses of the data—and to the reader, what you found during your analyses is the important material.

Additionally, short, concise quotes are better than long, repetitive quotes. This approach helps emphasize the story you're trying to tell and the argument you're trying to make. Also, don't be afraid to take quotations from multiple sources or places and edit them together to provide concise examples that really highlight the main points. For example, consider the passage and quotes in 2a from students.

(2a)   Each of these White teenagers shared their experiences with White privilege (all come from the *New York Times* article "What Students Are Saying about Race and Racism in America"):

I am white, and I live in a predominately white suburban town. I have never been treated differently for the color of my skin because I am a product of white privilege. I was not very politically active until George Floyd was murdered and the Black Lives Matter protests began in May. Since then, I've tried to better understand the hardships that people of color endure as a result of racism. I think it is of the utmost importance to speak out against corrupt systems, especially if you are not affected by these systems. Because in my opinion, choosing not to speak up against something because it does not involve you is proof that the system is working. Turning a blind eye with the thinly veiled excuse "politics isn't for me" can no longer mask selfish ignorance. This is not the time to be anti-political because silence is contributing to the blatant discrimination of black Americans. Hiding behind privilege instead of utilizing that very privilege to initiate change can no longer be justified.

—Annie, New Jersey

I think that this summer was really the first time that I was actually aware of the impact racism had. My parents have taught me, from a young age, that racism and injustice exist but I guess I did not understand to what extent. As a person who benefits from white privilege, I feel kind of guilty that I had not realized how it affected me before. Also, as a person who cannot yet vote, I am struggling to find ways that I can help make change. Do you have any suggestions?

—L, Pennsylvania

As a white person, I will never truly understand the horrors of being discriminated against for my skin color. I am privileged, not because of what I am, but because of what I'm not. The best thing I and other white people can do is listen and share. We will never completely know what racism will feel like, but we can listen and try to understand the pain of being harassed or attacked by the people who are supposed to protect you.

—Lindsay, North Carolina

Taken by themselves, each quote provides a detailed look into how the students are thinking about White privilege and their position, as

White teenagers, within a racial hierarchy. But even if your theme were "How White Students Think about Their White Privilege," there is a lot of additional information that could be cut and still provide sufficient evidence for that argument. A first step might be to revise the quotes as done in example 2b:

(2b)   Each of these White teenagers shared their experiences with White privilege:

> *I have never been treated differently for the color of my skin because I am a product of white privilege ... I think it is of the utmost importance to speak out against corrupt systems, especially if you are not affected by these systems ... choosing not to speak up against something because it does not involve you is proof that the system is working ... silence is contributing to the blatant discrimination of black Americans.*
>
> —Annie, New Jersey

> *My parents have taught me, from a young age, that racism and injustice exist but I guess I did not understand to what extent. As a person who benefits from white privilege, I feel kind of guilty that I had not realized how it affected me before ... {but} I am struggling to find ways that I can help make change.*
>
> —L, Pennsylvania

> *I will never truly understand the horrors of being discriminated against for my skin color. I am privileged, not because of what I am, but because of what I'm not. The best thing I and other white people can do is listen and share.*
>
> —Lindsay, North Carolina

Compared to the example in 2a, the example in 2b cut about half the words in the quotes but maintains the essential material needed to make claims about how White students think about their White privilege and position within a racial hierarchy. For instance, in the first quote above we cut out the following text:

- *I am white, and I live in a predominately white suburban town.* We cut this because all the participants we selected were White and living in a White suburban town wasn't necessary to convey the main points.
- *I was not very politically active until George Floyd was murdered and the Black Lives Matter protests began in May. Since then, I've tried to better understand the hardships that people of color endure as a result of*

racism. Although this is an autobiographically interesting quote, we needn't document the evolution of their thinking because we are interested in how students are thinking now. We could, however, use this material at another point in the manuscript: one that is devoted to change in White students' understanding of racial inequality over time, or one that focuses on factors that force students to face their own Whiteness and its unearned privileges.

- *Because in my opinion.* We cut this because the statement is clearly the respondent's own opinion.
- *Turning a blind eye with the thinly veiled excuse "politics isn't for me" can no longer mask selfish ignorance. This is not the time to be anti-political because silence is contributing to the blatant discrimination of black Americans.* We cut this because this is the respondent's views on what actions people should be taking now. Although we cut this here, it is another example of material that could be repurposed as evidence for another point elsewhere in the manuscript.

To really focus on your narrative, you could edit even further and add the storytelling approach we advocate, as was done in example 2c.

(2c)   Many White teenagers are aware of the benefits they reap from a system of racial inequality in the United States. They express things like "I have never been treated differently for the color of my skin because I am a product of white privilege" (Annie, New Jersey), "As a person who benefits from white privilege, I feel kind of guilty" (L, Pennsylvania), and "I am privileged, not because of what I am, but because of what I'm not" (Lindsay, North Carolina). They also have opinions on what White people may do to challenge racial oppression. They express things like "I think it is of the utmost importance to speak out against corrupt systems, especially if you are not affected by these systems … silence is contributing to the blatant discrimination of black Americans" (Annie) and "The best thing I and other white people can do is listen and share" (Lindsay). Others, however, are less sure of what to do. For example, L claimed they are "struggling to find ways that I can help."

Although the passage in example 2c is only 24 words shorter than the passage in example 2b, it is much clearer for the reader, in part because it has reorganized the quotes so they are presented around two or three sub-themes. Another way that it is clearer is that quotes are now presented from the storytelling approach; instead of having the quotes stand on their own as something to be processed by the reader, we've imbedded them into our narrative of the analyses.

A frequent challenge for ethnographic researchers is how to strike a balance between (a) doing justice to the people who provided their time and their stories to get the data for our analyses, and (b) providing the reader with a clear and concise report of the main themes and findings. However, it doesn't necessarily have to be an "either or" situation. One strategy would be to provide the clear and concise story telling approach exemplified in example 2c in the results section itself, but provide the fuller quotes, like those in either example 2a or example 2b, in an appendix or online supplement.

Exercise 6.3

For each item below, edit the three quotes into one paragraph with a storytelling approach like the one in example 2c.

1.* Three Women Guitar Players Reflecting on Being a Woman Guitar Player:

Starting back in 2000, I was not only a female guitar player in a world basically reserved for men but was also a European artist in the US and a Serbian artist as the first ever, trying to break into the blues guitar market in the USA. It required focus and determination, strong will and a vision of how my music would sound to set myself apart from the rest of the artists and carve my own recognizable sound.

—Ana Popovic, as quoted in Ehrenclou (2019)

I think the biggest challenge for a female musician is getting the respect from people, especially in the guitar world, where the biggest portion is for men. But I believe that, if you're good, you're good. It's all about your intention, and my intention is to make music and share it with people. I don't need to dress up a certain way to overcompensate my talent, I know my worth, I know how much I've been practicing, learning and grinding. My focus is on music. This way, people will respect you, whether you're a man or a woman.

—Mary N, as quoted in Female Rockers (2000)

Of course, if you look at statistics there is a so called gender problem. When I play in a band and there are other women besides me playing in it I take notice of course and it is a bit unusual. But in general I don't think too much about it. I got used so much to the fact that I'm mostly surrounded by male musicians. Probably a female car mechanic would feel the same. But it's getting more and more. I'm teaching at the "Hochschule für Musik" in Hamburg and nowadays there are already more female students then there used to be when I was studying. So it's also a question of time.

—Sandra Hempel, as quoted in Dupuis-Panther (n.d.)

2. Three professional athletes talking about dealing with mental health issues and addiction:

When I was swimming, the pool was my escape. I would take all that anger and use it as motivation. But now that escape is gone. I've learned in those moments it's important to try to take a step back. Take a deep breath. Go back to square one and ask yourself: Where these emotions are coming from? Why are you so angry? That's something I learned in treatment. That's something I try to teach my three boys. But when you're in that mood, you don't always want to do what's "right" or what you know you should do. I try to write notes on my mirror with a dry-erase marker. There are motivational quotes throughout my office I use to help me. And I journal. I have 20 to 30 pieces of scrap paper all over where I write things down that pop into my head or I want to remember to help me later.

—Michael Phelps, as quoted in Drehs (2000)

For athletes, you want to try to turn over every stone possible to be at the best of your ability. So if there's a doctor or counselor who can help you, why not turn over that stone? Having a culture conducive to mental health is big. I think we're getting there. Just about every (MLB) team has a psychology department. I'm glad we're starting to understand. We're all human, and I think the more we talk about mental health, the better.

—Rick Ankiel, as quoted in Gleeson and Brady (2017)

I think that hiding and not talking about this is the kiss of death for all addicts that are dealing with their issues, that haven't gotten help, that haven't gone into recovery. My recovery started the second

> *I was able to not just admit that I had a problem, but actually talk about it with the people around me, and to be brutally honest and not lie about how many drinks I had and not lessen the magnitude of the pain I was in. Once I started to get really truthful and really honest, that's when I really started to get and seek out the help I really needed. So the truth is the thing that kinda set me free, and then of course my family and my loved ones. Those are the people that have helped me through this process the most.*
>
> —Abby Wambach, as quoted in Van Amburg (2016)

Findings from Multiple Regression Research

In regression, hypotheses usually concern relations between and among variables. Such hypotheses are often tested by determining whether coefficients differ significantly from 0. For example, imagine a study in which we're interested in the link between education and confidence that all mail-in and absentee ballots were counted in the 2020 US Presidential election. We hypothesize that being less educated is associated with less confidence that all mail-in and absentee ballots were counted. In other words, these variables should be correlated negatively. We measure these variables along with race/ethnicity, age, and gender (because of the possibility that these latter variables may covary with confidence that all mail-in and absentee ballots were counted in the 2020 election). The results of the study are shown in Table 6.3, on page 93.

A description of these findings in statisticalese appears in passage 3a:

(3a)   Regression results are in Table 6.3 Compared to having a college degree, having completed some college (logit coefficient = -0.857, $p < 0.001$) and having a high school degree (logit coefficient = -1.033, $p < 0.001$) were negatively correlated with confidence that all mail-in and absentee ballots were counted. Relative to Whites, being Black (logit coefficient = 1.387, $p < 0.001$) or Hispanic (logit coefficient = 0.483, $p < 0.001$) was positively correlated with confidence that all mail-in and absentee ballots were counted. Age was positively correlated with confidence that all mail-in and absentee ballots were counted (logit coefficient = 0.003, $p < 0.001$). Finally, relative to identifying as a man, both identifying as a woman (logit coefficient = 0.138, $p < 0.001$) or identifying as a non-binary gender (logit coefficient = 0.671, p < 0.001) were positively associated with confidence that all mail-in and absentee ballots were counted.

This passage has several problems. First, it repeats most of the information in the table, a practice that makes one wonder why the author included the table. Second, the passage ignores the hypotheses and the reasons why variables were included in the study. The critical statistical relationship is between education and confidence that all mail-in and absentee ballots were counted; the others were control variables and were computed simply to be sure the correlation between education and confidence that all mail-in and absentee ballots were counted does not reflect the impact of a third variable.

Passage 3b describes the same regression coefficients but in a story-telling mode:

(3b)   Results from a logistic regression analysis of confidence that all mail-in and absentee ballots were counted on education, race/ethnicity, age, and gender are shown in Table 6.3. As predicted, net of controls, lower education was associated with lower confidence that all mail-in and absentee ballots were counted.

Passage 3b begins with the critical correlation but emphasizes the relation between the variables, not the fact that the regression coefficient is significant.

In passage 3b, the description is variable oriented; passage 3c describes the same regression coefficients but in terms of subjects' characteristics:

(3c)   Results from a logistic regression analysis of confidence that all mail-in and absentee ballots were counted on education, race/ethnicity, age, and gender are shown in Table 6.3. As predicted, individuals with high school education or some college experience had lower odds than those with a college degree of having confidence that all mail-in and absentee ballots were counted in the 2020.

A subject-oriented description is rooted in concrete characteristics about the subjects, making it clearer than a more abstract variable-oriented description. But sometimes passages about describing characteristics get long and clumsy. In those cases, the variable-oriented description may be more effective. But be consistent; don't mix the two modes.

Exercise 6.4

Rewrite these passages so they are story oriented, not statistics oriented.

1. Background: This study was designed to assess change in women's average work week (in hours) between 2000 and 2021. The hypothesis is that women's work week will have increased over the study period.

Description of results: OLS regression results are shown in Table 6.4. Year was positively associated with typical hours worked in a week among women (b = 0.041, $p < 0.001$). The number of children a person has was negatively correlated with typical hours worked in a week among women (b = -0.202, $p < 0.001$). Relative to married women, being a previously married woman was positively associated with typical hours worked in a week whereas being a never married woman was negatively associated with typical hours worked in a week (b = 1.243 and -3.430, respectively, $p < 0.001$). Finally, compared to being a White woman, being a Black woman

Table 6.4 OLS Regression Analysis of Typical Hours Worked in a Week among Women

	b/se
Year	0.041***
	(0.002)
Number of Children	-0.202***
	(0.011)
Divorced/Separated/Widowed[b]	1.243***
	(0.032)
Never Married[b]	-3.430***
	(0.030)
Black[a]	2.263***
	(0.036)
Intercept	-46.703***
	(3.907)
r-squared	.023

*$p < .05$, **$p < .01$, ***$p < .001$ (N = 958,194; reference categories are [a] = White and [b] = Married)

was positively associated with typical hours worked in a week ($b = 2.263, p < 0.001$).

2. Background: This study was designed to assess whether type of veteran status (i.e. non-veteran, wartime veteran, and peace-time veteran) is associated with becoming incarcerated. The hypothesis is that both being a wartime veteran and peace-time veteran will be associated with increased odds of becoming incarcerated.

Description of results: results from a logistic regression analysis of whether someone was incarcerated are shown in Table 6.5. In this model, being a wartime veteran was negatively associated with becoming incarcerated (relative to non-veterans; logit coefficient = -0.767. $p < 0.001$), but being a peacetime veteran was not significantly associated with becoming incarcerated (again, relative to non-veterans). Both age (logit coefficient = -0.044. $p < 0.001$)

Table 6.5 Logistic Regression of Becoming Incarcerated

	b/se
Wartime Veteran[a]	−0.767***
	(0.032)
Non-wartime Veteran[a]	0.037
	(0.038)
Age	−0.044***
	(0.001)
Women[b]	−1.146***
	(0.021)
High School[c]	−0.772***
	(0.019)
Some College[c]	−3.386***
	(0.051)
College[c]	−2.727***
	(0.053)
Constant	−0.186***
	(0.033)
Pseudo r-squared	0.32

***$p < .001$ (N = 105,802; reference categories are [a] = Non-veteran, [b] = Men, and [c] = Less than High School) and being a woman (logit coefficient = -1.146. $p < 0.001$) were negatively associated with becoming incarcerated. Relative to not completing a high school degree, a high school degree, some college, and a college degree were all negatively associated with becoming incarcerated (logit coefficients = -0.772, -3.386, and -2.727, respectively; $p < 0.001$).

3.* Background: this study was designed to assess the associations between the percentage of Black and Hispanics adults living in a state, and the state's incarceration rate for marijuana possession. The hypotheses are that (H_1) states where a greater percentage of the population is Black will have higher incarceration rates for marijuana possession and (H_2) states where a greater percentage of the population is Hispanic will have higher incarceration rates for marijuana possession.

Description of results: results from OLS models regressing states' incarceration rates on state level covariates are shown in Table 6.6. The percent of the state that is Black is positively associated with

Table 6.6 OLS Regression of States' Incarceration Rates for Marijuana Possession

	b/se
% Black	737.2**
	(137.2)
% Hispanic	133.9
	(98.0)
West[a]	397.1**
	(72.0)
Northeast[a]	263.1*
	(99.3)
South[a]	13.7
	(12.9)
Population	14.9
	(98.4)
Poverty rate	57.6*
	(29.3)

*$p < .05$, **$p < .01$, ***$p < .001$ (N = 200; reference categories are [a] = Midwest State)

states' incarceration rates for marijuana possession (b = 737.2, $p < 0.01$), but the percent of the state that is Hispanic was not significantly associated with states' incarceration rates for marijuana possession. Relative to the Midwest, being a state in the West or Northeast was positively associated with states' incarceration rates for marijuana possession (b = 397.1, $p < 0.01$; and $p = 263.1$, $p < 0.05$, respectively), but being a state in the South did not have an independent association with states' incarceration rates for marijuana possession. Although a states' overall population size was not significantly associated with states' incarceration rates for marijuana possession, state poverty rate was positively associated with states' incarceration rates for marijuana possession (b = 57.6, $p < 29.3$).

Assembling the Pieces

After you've described the key themes and findings, you may need to describe other unexpected results. For example, when analyzing your ethnographic data, you may uncover results in your analyses that are unrelated to main themes or your main argument but are important to share. It is perfectly appropriate to add a brief paragraph toward the end of the results section to report these additional findings. For example, maybe you were doing an ethnographic study to understand gender performance among women firefighters, but discovered during your analyses an important finding regarding the gender performance of men fighters working along women firefighters. Sentence 5 provides an example of how you could write about this in your results section.

(5)   While analyzing the data, an unexpected theme emerged: women who worked in firehouses that were otherwise exclusively men commented that men would increase their performance of masculinity by commenting about "how exciting it was to be risking their lives" or sometimes being "extremely confrontational" with bystanders at fires. In contrast, women who worked in firehouses that included at least one other woman reported the men in the

firehouse were advocates of women firefighters: the firehouses made intentional efforts to recruit additional female firefighters, and "provided encouragement and support for me to apply for promotions, and challenged the now-ex-Chief when he questioned if I was really ready to be Captain."

Similarly, multiple regression analysis may reveal an unanticipated but newsworthy finding. For example, sentence 6 documents an unexpected finding regarding racial differences in the transition from fulltime work into part time work or full retirement:

(6)   Analyses showed that although no racial differences were observed initially, once the models adjusted for caregiving responsibilities, Black workers were more likely than White workers to transition to partial retirement (instead of full retirement) (OR = 1.414, $p < .01$).

You may also need to report the findings of ancillary analyses. These typically are not of interest substantively but provide evidence about the robustness or sensitivity of the main analyses. For example, passage 7 provides the results of an ancillary analysis documenting that the findings reported in Table 6.3 were robust when education and race/ethnicity were operationalized differently.

(7)   To verify the robustness of our findings, we estimated a number of additional models to assess whether our findings were sensitive to how we choose to measure education and race/ethnicity. For instance, we estimated a model where education was measured in years (instead of categories), and race (White and Black) and ethnicity (Hispanic and non-Hispanic) were treated separately (instead of an aggregate measure of race/ethnicity). Regardless of how education and race/ethnicity were specified, the substantive findings remained unchanged.

With the primary and ancillary analyses described, you can piece everything together. We recommend you begin with the ancillary findings and then move to the main results. Just as a pop concert starts with opening acts and ends with featured performer, it's always better to build momentum and end strong. We suggest you describe this organization in a brief paragraph at the beginning of the results section. This paragraph also allows you to describe information you don't want to repeat over and over. For example, rather than repeat "$p < .05$" dozens of times, you could include the phrase, "For effects described as significant, $p < .05$." Similarly, there may be effects of interest that were never significant in any analyses. Rather than say so repeatedly, say it once in this paragraph: "In the analyses reported here, education was never significantly associated with any other variables." Passage 8 illustrates this sort of introductory paragraph:

(8)   Results
      The results are reported in two sections—one devoted to analyses of the structure of the emotion tasks and another devoted to links between performance on those tasks and participants' sense of agency. Preliminary analyses revealed comparable performance for men and women; consequently, this variable is not discussed further. Unless noted to the contrary, for all effects described as significant, $p < .01$.

A final note: Some writers are nervous about reporting their results in the economical manner we've described here. They fear reviewers may find fault with this lean style of reporting. Fortunately, there's an easy solution that can satisfy the needs of reviewers and some readers for details of analyses and the needs of most readers for a strong story line that doesn't run aground in a sea of quotations or multiple regression analyses. As we've suggested a few times previously in this lesson, write the results in storytelling mode, but prepare a supplementary document that includes all the details. Most journals are happy to make such information available to reviewers and to publish it online if the article is accepted. Thus, the details are available to those who want them but don't disrupt the flow for everyone else.

Wrap Up

1. Identify the key themes and findings of your work—the ones worth reporting to the scientific community and support the story you are trying to tell in this report —and decide whether they are best depicted in a graph or a table.

2. Describe each primary theme or outcome briefly, telling a story with a minimal amount of qualitative or statistical detail.
3. Begin the results section with a brief orienting paragraph, comment on important ancillary themes and analyses (but feel free to house the results supporting those analyses in an online supplement), and end with the main theme findings (saving the best for last).

For Practice

1. Look for ethnographic research; decide whether the subheadings give a clear and concise indication of the themes that come after them. If they don't, rewrite them so they do.
2. Look for graphs and tables; decide whether each is the appropriate format for reporting the data.
3. Find results sections that are written to focus on quotes; rewrite in storytelling mode emphasizing themes.
4. Find results sections that are written in statisticalese; rewrite in storytelling mode emphasizing findings.
5. Look for results sections that lead with the main findings and end with the ancillary findings. Do these seem to end with a whimper instead of a bang?

ANSWERS TO EXERCISES

Exercise 6.1

2. While the example subheading in 2b provides a clear descriptive placeholder for the results that will come after, it doesn't say anything about how Asian American women are participating in social justice rallies. In contrast, the subheading in 2a highlights that Asian American women are more active in social justice rallies.
3. While the example subheading in 3a provides a clear descriptive placeholder for the results that will come after, it doesn't tell us anything about how adults make sense of growing up with a depressed parent. In contrast, the subheading in 3b describes some of the ways that people feel like growing up with a depressed parent shapes their lives as adults.

Exercise 6.2

1. This is more easily shown in a figure.

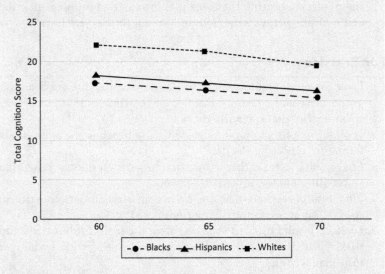

Figure 6.2 Change in Overall Cognition by Race and Age.

2. This can be presented easily in a table. Table 6.7 is an illustrative example.

Table 6.7 OLS Regression Results of Percentage of Network That Is Composed of Friends

	Men	Women
Married[a]	−30.1*	−20.2*
Age	−01.2	01.5
Education (Years)	2.2	−7.1
Not Currently Working[b]	0.7	−14.7*
Good Health	2.4	−3.1
r-squared	0.08	0.09

*p < .05, **p < .01, ***p < .01 (N = 3,553; reference categories are [a] = Unmarried and [b] = Currently Working)

Exercise 6.3

2. Professional athletes often connect their mental health issues and addiction to their sport. Some use their sport as way to cope with their mental health issues. For instance, Michael Phelps recalled that "[w]hen I was swimming, the pool was my escape. I would take all that anger and use it as motivation." Other athletes leverage their desire to be great at their sport into justification to get mental health treatment. For example, Rick Ankiel thinks that if there's a doctor or counselor who can help you, why not use that resource to "be at the best of your ability."

But athletes also talk about addressing their mental health and addiction challenges outside of the sport. Abby Wambach recalls "my recovery started the second I was able ... to admit that I had a problem ... [and] actually talk about it with the people around me, and to be brutally honest and not lie [about it]" and that "my family and my loved ones ... are the people that have helped me through this the most." Phelps talks about how, since retiring, he uses "motivational quotes" and journaling to "take a step back ... [and] get back to square one."

Exercise 6.4

1. OLS regression results are shown in Table 6.4. As predicted, women's average work week increased by 0.041 hours a year, such that between 2000 and 2021, the average woman's work increased by 0.861 hours. [OR write as "... increased by nearly one hour each week."]

2. Logistic regression results are shown in Table 6.5. As expected, peacetime veterans were more likely to end up incarcerated than non-veterans. Contrary to the hypothesis, however, wartime veterans were less likely than non-veterans to end up incarcerated.

Lesson 7

Discussing Your Findings

Lesson Outline

- Some common mistakes
- A template for a successful discussion section
- Ending strong

Having completed an introduction and a results section, you're nearly done! All that's left is the discussion. This section has a simple purpose: to consider the issues raised in the introduction in light of the results of your work. In other words, your research was designed to explore a new idea or to answer questions; here is where you explain what you found during your exploration or how you answered your questions, and where you tell readers how your themes coalesce into a new idea or what the findings mean.

Writers often struggle with this section, in part because it lacks a well-defined structure. Thus, in this last lesson, we start by looking at some problems commonly encountered in discussion sections and then consider some solutions to those problems. We finish the lesson with some tips for ending your paper with a bang!

Some Common Mistakes

Let's start with a six-pack of problems common to discussion sections.

- *Too long*: some authors feel compelled to talk about every single result, including, for example, the unexpected, uninteresting four-way interaction that probably won't be replicated. Or they feel obligated to discuss every conceivable shortcoming in their work. Don't! The discussion is a place to say something valuable about a

DOI: 10.4324/9781003328285-7

few major topics, not to write ad nauseam about every topic that's even remotely related to the study.

- *Poorly organized*: too often discussion sections seem to be written in stream-of-consciousness mode: ideas appear without any obvious order or relation to each other. Said differently, it's as if the author wrote one paragraph about each of five different ideas and then ordered those five paragraphs randomly. The paragraphs aren't linked together, and the discussion has no overall plan.

- *Doesn't discuss*: some authors fill the discussion with a detailed review of the results but don't actually discuss them. A summary of key findings is an excellent way to begin a discussion, but then you need to put those findings in perspective for the reader, explaining what conclusions they warrant and what questions remain unanswered.

- *Off topic*: writers often have opinions about a general area of research, and they sometimes use the discussion to get these thoughts "off their chest"—even when they're only remotely related to the study being reported. Of course, if your findings have broader implications for the field, feel free to mention them. But having written six solid paragraphs on relevant topics does not give you license to go off topic in the seventh paragraph.

- *Inconsistent or inappropriate tone*: in Lesson 2 we considered the importance of writing in a voice that balances hedges and intensifiers so that your writing seems self-assured without seeming arrogant. Nowhere is this more important than in the discussion. As you describe how your findings address the issues that motivated the study, you don't want to seem too pushy or too dismissive of other relevant work. Yet you shouldn't be overly cautious—hedging everything—because readers won't believe your conclusions if you don't seem to believe them yourself! To achieve the desired cautiously confident voice, use the strategy described in Lesson 2: write a draft without any hedges or intensifiers, then add hedges and intensifiers as needed, with more of the former than the latter.

- *Too much self-praise*: too often authors fill their discussion with phrases such as "We are the first to show ..." or "These findings are important because ..." It's as if the author doubts the reader will believe the findings are sufficiently innovative or important and resorts to these phrases to convince the reader of the study's value. The place to make the case for a study is in the introduction: a clear and compelling rationale for the study should make it obvious how the work is innovative and valuable; you needn't waste words reminding the reader that "we're first!" or trying to convince the reader "This really is important!"

Except for self-praise, these problems stem from the lack of a well-defined structure for the discussion. An effective plan to guide your writing usually eliminates problems of length, organization, and inappropriate topics. The next section provides a handy template for writing a discussion.

Exercise 7.1

A good organization won't eliminate the problem of self-praise in a discussion, so you need to be able to recognize such writing and purge it. Which of the following sentences seem guilty of self-praise?

1. These findings support the hypothesis that some companies use multiple identities to hide their predatory behavior.
2. The results reported here are rich in their implications for the literature on racial and educational differences in incarceration for violent crime.
3. This study is the first attempt to determine the role of housing equity on cross-national differences in wealth inequality.
4. The findings from our social network analyses complement the analyses of narratives in showing that older inmates are more powerful and more influential.
5. The ground-breaking contribution of the present work is in demonstrating that the likelihood of marital infidelity is affected by the relative incomes of husbands and wives.
6. This finding is particularly valuable in identifying the causal impact on violence crime of local non-profit organizations that focus on crime and community life.

A Template for a Successful Discussion Section

You can avoid many of the problems that bedevil discussion sections by using the template shown in Table 7.1. Because the structure of a discussion section can vary depending on the study, begin this section

Table 7.1 A Template for a Discussion Section

Section	Purpose
Introductory paragraph	Provides a summary of the findings and an overview of the rest of the discussion.
Limiting conditions	Describes features of the study that limit the conclusions that can be drawn.
Study-specific issues, 1–3	Discuss the issues central to the study as well as unexpected but provocative findings.
Implications for X	Discuss the implications of the findings for social policy, treatment, or instruction.
General implications	Link the findings to more general concerns and issues associated with the area of research.

with a brief orienting paragraph. It should contain one to three sentences in which you review the key findings of your work; if you have more than three sentences, you're probably going into too much detail. Then include one or two sentences in which you provide an overview of the rest of the discussion, an overview that's linked to the subheadings used in the rest of the discussion. Passage 1 shows an illustrative orienting paragraph.

(1)   Drawing upon data from 16 nations, we showed that occupational segregation by gender is lower in countries that provide maternity leave and greater in countries that pass anti-discrimination legislation. In the remainder of this discussion, we begin by considering some limiting conditions on the evidence. Then we discuss the mechanisms by which maternity leave may reduce gender segregation. Finally, we explore the unexpected outcome that anti-discrimination legislation increased gender segregation.

This orienting paragraph leads the reader to expect three main sections, one on limiting conditions on the evidence, a second on the way that maternity leave reduces gender segregation, and a third on the impact of anti-discrimination legislation on gender segregation; each will be introduced with a subheading.

The orienting paragraph is then followed by several elements, each introduced with a subheading.

- *Limiting conditions*: start by considering the features of the research that may limit the conclusions able to be drawn from the findings. This is not "confession" time where you list each blemish in your work. Nor is it the place to rationalize weak data or serious flaws. (If your work has unconvincing data or fatal flaws, don't try to rescue the work in the discussion; do a better study.) Instead, mention reasons why your work is not the "last word" on the topic. Passage 2 refers to the study in passage 1 to illustrate this kind of paragraph.

(2)   Two features of this work limit the conclusions we can draw about cross-national differences in occupational segregation by gender. First, the study involved only developing nations; whether the findings would also hold for developed nations is an open question. Second, our measures of maternity leave and anti-discrimination legislation were dichotomous (present vs absent). Our measure of maternity leave ignored differences in the quality and quantity of maternity leave across nations and our measure of anti-discrimination legislation ignored enforcement of that legislation. More detailed measurement of these constructs would allow us to better describe cross-national differences in occupational segregation by gender.

- *Study-specific issues*: next discuss one to three issues specific to the study. Most of these will be linked to the rationale for the study. This is your chance to explain how your findings yield greater understanding of the phenomena that motivated your work. Of course, sometimes studies yield unanticipated but provocative findings; these could be examined under one of the study-specific headings. Passage 3 illustrates a paragraph dealing with an issue from the study mentioned in passages 1 and 2.

(3)   An unexpected outcome was that occupational segregation by gender was greater in countries that had passed anti-discrimination legislation. This result may reflect the fact that countries with greater segregation are more likely to pass anti-discrimination legislation. Another interpretation is that anti-discrimination laws increase participation of women in the workforce but they end up primarily in service occupations that already

are dominated by women. Distinguishing these outcomes will require longitudinal analyses.

- *Implications for*: often findings from research have implications for social policy, intervention, or instruction. Use this section to explain the impact of your findings on, for example, policies toward military families or treatment for people with depression. However, avoid the temptation to make a statement about implications for social policy, intervention, or instruction if the "implication" isn't well connected to your results. Said differently, some writers feel compelled to put a policy implication in every report they write; however, you should make a statement about policy implications only when your research has clear implications for policy. Passage 4 shows part of a paragraph dealing with the implications of findings for public health.

(4) The present findings also have implications for public health, specifically, with respect to ways to reduce the number of communities in which parents refuse to vaccinate their children. Our findings suggest that interventions to encourage parents to vaccinate their children must consider reasons why parents are initially attracted to such communities. Additionally, to succeed, interventions must change parents' beliefs that (a) refusing to vaccinate children is a sign of "good parenting" and (b) vaccination is a risky event for their children.

- *General implications*: link the study to more general concerns in the area of research. This is your opportunity to show how your work is relevant to a broader range of issues and thus is of interest to more than a handful of experts. For example, the authors of the study described in passage 1 might link their findings to other topics in the study of occupational segregation by gender and gender discrimination in the workplace. Passage 5 illustrates the beginning of a paragraph discussing the implications of the study cited in passage 10 of Lesson 5:

(5) More generally, the present findings contribute to a more nuanced view of the educational trajectories and educational outcomes for transgender students. Contrary to previous findings that transgender students are less likely to enroll in college,

we find that, after adjusting for region, transgender students are more likely to enroll in college. Not only does this finding have important implications for the kinds of interventions that would be most effective at increasing college enrollment among transgender students, it draws into questions findings based on community studies of transgender students. In short, we need more national level data on transgender students to effectively understand the ways in which their lives are similar and different from their cisgender peers.

This paragraph takes a step back and puts the findings concerning educational achievements of transgender children in the broader perspective of the lives of transgender students.

The elements of this template provide a starting point you can tailor to suit the needs of your paper. If you're reporting a simple, straightforward study, a five-paragraph discussion might be perfectly adequate—one paragraph each for orientation, limiting conditions, two issues, and implications. If, instead, you're reporting a half dozen studies, you might begin the discussion with a paragraph entitled "Summary of Findings." And not every study will have implications for social policy, intervention, or instruction, so that section could be deleted. The point is simple: make the template your own, adjusting it fit each manuscript that you write.

Regardless of the variations you introduce, by starting with this template, you'll avoid the first four common problems listed on pages 112–113. The template provides focus and structure, so that the discussion won't be too long but will be organized, discuss the issues at hand, and stay on topic.

Finally, two features of this template may seem at odds with research reports you've read. First, some authors discuss limiting conditions toward the end of the discussion, but we think that's less effective. The rule that sentences should end strong also applies to the entire discussion section. Get the limiting conditions out of the way and then move to the provocative aspects of your work, building momentum as you go.

Second, there is no section titled "Directions for Future Research." Of course, you should point to the kinds of studies needed, but those recommendations are more compelling when they appear in the context of specific, unanswered questions. For example, the authors of passage 3 suggested that longitudinal studies would help to distinguish different interpretations of their findings; fleshing out that suggestion is more constructive if presented in conjunction with their explanation instead of in a separate section.

Exercise 7.2

Find a published article in which the discussion lacks subheadings. Identify the function of each paragraph—summary of findings and overview, limiting conditions, study-specific issues, and general implications. Are there paragraphs that have other functions? If the discussion doesn't have an orienting paragraph, write one.

Exercise 7.3

For each of the studies described in Exercise 5.4 on pages 85–86, identify one limiting condition that could be described, as well as one study-specific issue.

Ending Strong

Your paper needs to end with a bang, not a whimper. Although not all journals require that you have a formal conclusion section, you should write a strong conclusion. Avoid banal endings like those in sentences 6 and 7 that simply call for more research:

(6)   Future research on this phenomenon is essential.

(7)   Answering these lingering questions is a topic for future research.

These sentences apply to nearly all research so they add nothing meaningful. Instead, aim for a memorable ending whose take-home message makes readers believe the time spent on your article was well invested.

A first step in writing a strong ending is identifying the take-home message and a vivid way of conveying it. You can think of this like the chorus to a pop song: you want it catchy and memorable enough that people sing it in the shower. Often the solution is readily available: the hook you used to grab the reader's attention in the introduction. Lesson 5 mentions several ways to get readers to sit up and take notice: an interesting behavior, a rhetorical question, an intriguing statistic, an anecdote, or a quote. These hooks often can be the basis for a powerful ending. In fact, you should select a hook in the first place based, in part, on its value in setting up a strong ending. For example, Lesson 5 included these five examples of hooks:

(8)   People often complete forms in which they are asked to specify their race. Completing these forms can be challenging for biracial people because they are often forced to choose one race. Although this situation is common, we know little about how biracial people select labels to describe themselves.

(9)   Suppose your young child accidently broke a prized family heirloom. Would you send them to their room as punishment or would you explain to them why they should be more careful next time? Research on the influence of culture on parenting choices suggests you have a variety of culturally appropriate parenting decisions you could make, but there is little evidence regarding how you would select between competing alternatives (Jones et al., 2015).

(10)   Approximately 90% of the published articles on adolescents' friendships report research conducted in schools where at least 60% of the students are White. This is problematic for research on racial variation in friendships because most Black and Hispanic students attend schools in which White students are in the minority (Irwin et al., 2021).

(11)   In 2017, more than 80 women—including Angelina Jolie, Mira Sorvino, and Gwyneth Paltrow—came forward to accuse movie producer and studio head Harvey Weinstein of sexual assault. Weinstein's trial was front page news and resulted in a conviction and a 23-year prison sentence. His victims' experiences are far too common: nearly a third of all women report experiencing sexual harassment at their place of work (Kearl, 2018).

(12)   "I grew up in the church. I loved the church. I studied to be a pastor. I worked as an associate pastor. But when the leaders rejected One Church Plan and voted in favor of the Traditional Plan, I had to leave. I was devastated. I felt betrayed. I let the church into my heart, and they rejected me because I'm a man who just happens to love another man." This man's experience suggests that some congregations are not open to homosexuality, but in fact little is known about the ways in which homosexual men and women who grew up in the church attempt to reconcile the tensions between their sexual identity and their religious identity.

The starting point for a strong ending is to return to the hook, updating it in light of your findings. For example, suppose the study mentioned in passage 8 showed that two factors influence the racial labels that biracial individuals chose. Sentence 13 shows an ending that highlights the take-home message by citing the hook from the introduction:

(13a)   Thus, the present findings indicate that biracial individuals pick racial labels based on contextual cues and the strength of their identification with each race. The results also lead to practical advice: forms such as applications and questionnaires will be most accurate when they do not include cues that would trigger any racial identity and when biracial people can select multiple racial labels that they can weight.

Sentence 14 illustrates use of the hook from passage 12:

(14)   The work reported confirms that the man's experiences described in the opening vignette are common: lesbian, gay, and bisexual people are often rejected by their churches and, consequently, they either (a) remain with the church but delegitimize church leaders who preach anti-gay messages, or (b) search for a new church that is more welcoming.

Exercise 7.4

Use the hooks you created in Exercise 5.1 (or the ones we suggested on page 87) to write a paper-ending sentence. For the first study, assume that paid employment remains an important source of people's identity. For the second study, assume that educating Millennials about the need to save for retirement is effective but that requiring them to contribute 7% of their income every month is more effective. For the third study, assume that, overall, 17% young adults who work in professional occupations found their job through an acquaintance of a family member, but that this was more common among middle-class young adults (26%) than among lower-class young adults (8%).

To underscore the conclusions you want readers to take away from your paper, consider the techniques for emphasis mentioned in Lesson 2: using *it*, *there*, and *what* to shift text to the end of the sentence and *not only X but Y* to highlight new findings. For example, a manuscript's end is a great place to use *what*, as illustrated in sentence 12b.

(13b) What stands out in this work is that biracial individuals pick racial labels based on contextual cues and the strength of their identification with each race. The results also lead to practical advice:

If previous findings had revealed the importance of contextual cues but strength of racial identification was new in the present study, then you could use *not only X but Y* as in sentence 12c:

(13c) Thus, the present findings indicate that biracial individuals pick racial labels based not only on contextual cues but also on the strength of their identification with each race. The results also lead to practical advice:

You could even combine *what* with *not only X but Y* as in passage 13d:

(13d) What stands out in this work is that biracial individuals pick racial labels based not only on contextual cues but also on the strength of their identification with each race. The results also lead to practical advice:

One other useful tool for emphasizing your take-home message is the **periodic sentence**. We didn't mention this kind of sentence earlier because periodic sentences can be so over the top that they aren't appropriate for routine emphasis. But they can be a wonderful way to end a paper.

Periodic sentences have two essential components. The first is an introductory clause that's much longer than average—exactly the kind of clause that Lesson 1 urges you to eliminate. The second defining element is a word that's repeated, sometimes several times, in the introductory clause. Passage 14 illustrates a famous periodic sentence:

(14) "But when you have seen vicious mobs lynch your mothers and fathers at will and drown your sisters and brothers at whim; when you have seen hate-filled policemen curse, kick and even kill your

black brothers and sisters; when you see the vast majority of your twenty million Negro brothers smothering in an airtight cage of poverty in the midst of an affluent society … then you will understand why we find it difficult to wait."

This sentence, taken from Martin Luther King, Jr's (1994) second "Letter from the Birmingham Jail," begins with a long introductory clause in which *when* is repeated three times (ten times in the unedited version!); both the length of the clause and the repeated *when* get the reader's attention.

In a discussion section, a periodic sentence is a great way to summarize your evidence and restate the critical conclusion. That is, you present the evidence in the long introductory clause and the conclusion in the briefer main clause, as in sentence 15:

(15)   Given that unions are relatively weak in the United States, given that workers who are less skilled and low paid are less likely to be unionized, and given that unions benefit individuals but poverty affects entire households, we anticipated that unionization would not reduce working poverty.

The 38-word introductory clause summarizes the evidence, introducing each finding with *given*; the nine-word main clause provides the conclusion that follows from that evidence. Periodic sentences could also be built around repetition of *because, when,* or *considering,* with each introducing a piece of evidence that supports the conclusion.

Finally, if you want to pull out all the stops, this is a great place to spice up your writing as described in the second part of Lesson 3. Figures of speech (e.g., metaphor, antimetabole) and neologisms capture the reader's attention wherever they appear, a feature that makes them especially well-suited to end your discussion. For example, sentence 16 illustrates use of antimetabole to highlight findings from work on training aggressive youth to recognize facial emotions:

(16)   When aggressive youth recognize anger in a face, they are better able to face their own anger.

And sentence 17 shows how a new word created by adding a suffix can punch up a conclusion:

(17)   What stands out in each study is the number of property managers who repeatedly evict a household from the same address; such evictaholic managers account for nearly half of all eviction filings.

By combining these techniques for spiced-up writing with the hook from the introduction and techniques for emphasis, you can end your paper on a high note. This ending—along with a goose-bump-inducing introduction and a results section with a strong story line—is likely to make readers believe your article is exceptional and well worth reading.

Exercise 7.5

Use techniques for emphasis and spicy writing to improve the conclusions you wrote for Exercise 7.4.

Wrap Up

1. Avoid common problems of discussion sections, which include being too long and poorly organized, rehashing but not discussing results, wandering off topic, using an inappropriate tone, and indulging in self-praise.
2. A useful organization for a discussion section begins with an orienting paragraph (review of findings and overview of the rest of the section), followed by sections devoted to limiting conditions, a few study-specific issues, and general implications.
3. End strong by applying techniques for emphasis.

For Practice

1. Scan the discussion section of several articles for the six common problems described on pages 112–114.
2. Find an article in which the discussion section has no headings; revise the text using the template provided in this chapter.
3. Find an article that ends in a whimper. Revise it to provide the bang.

ANSWERS TO EXERCISES

Exercise 7.1

The following sentences have self-praise (in italics).

2. The results reported here are *rich* in their implications for the literature on occupational segregation by gender.
3. This study is the *first attempt* to determine the role of housing equity on cross-national differences in wealth inequality.
5. The *ground-breaking* contribution of the present work is in demonstrating that the likelihood of marital infidelity is affected by the relative incomes of husbands and wives.
6. This finding is *particularly valuable* in identifying the causal impact on violence crime of local non-profit organizations that focus on crime and community life.

Exercise 7.3

1. One limiting condition would be that the findings apply only to Asian men in the United States. Would the findings apply to Asian men in other countries who aspire to coach? A study-specific issue would be the extent to which similar findings may occur when Asian men aspire to leadership roles outside of coaching.
2. One limiting condition would be that 92% of the women in the sample were White; whether the findings would apply to women of other races is an open question. A study-specific issue would be the mechanisms that explain why the pace of inroads into occupations held by men is not the same for college-educated and non-college-educated women.

Exercise 7.4

1. The present findings demonstrate that, despite the COVID-19 pandemic, paid employment remains an essential part of people's identity. Even while wearing masks, people meeting others are likely to say, "What do you do?"
2. Based on the present work, if Millennials are to avoid the catastrophe of reaching retirement age with no funds,

requiring them to save a substantial amount of their income every month is the best intervention.

3. The results report here identify one of the ways that social class differences replicate: children like Ben, the son of the middle-class accountant in the opening vignette, are better able to take advantage of their parents' social networks to secure professional jobs of their own.

Exercise 7.5

1. What stands out in this work is that, despite the COVID-19 pandemic, paid employment remains an essential part of people's identity. Even while wearing masks, people meeting others are likely to say, "What do you do?"

2. Based on the present work, if Millennials are to avoid the catastrophe of reaching retirement age with no funds, not only educating them but also requiring them to save a substantial amount of their income every month are effective intervention.

3. The results reported here identify one of the ways that social class differences replicate: children like Ben, the son of the middle-class accountant in the opening vignette, often rely on a connecting-with-others-through-a-parent's-network strategy to secure professional jobs of their own.

Epilogue
The end of the book, but the beginning of your writing journey

Part 1 Finishing Touches
Part 2 From Principles to Practices

For sociologists, writing is the primary way we share our ideas. And sharing ideas effectively is vital because many of those ideas are intended to make the world a more just, equal, and better place. To help you share more effectively, the aim of the seven lessons in this book has been to provide you with the tools to write more clearly and more effectively.

But at this point you may feel as if we've missed some important things. For example, why is there no lesson on writing a method section? And, although you may like many of the tips that we've suggested, you may feel overwhelmed at the prospect of implementing all of them the next time that you write. In this epilogue, we address both concerns.

Finishing Touches

Why isn't there a lesson on writing a method section? Or on writing a good abstract? The main reason is that we wanted to keep the book comparatively short and thus we focused on critical tips that contribute to a successful manuscript. Most introductory books on common styles (e.g., APA, MLA, or ASA) have basic information about how to write a title, abstract, and method section; frankly, there's not much left to say. So, what follows are a few suggestions for writing these elements of your manuscript.

The Title

A title is the first part of your article a reader sees, and it's part of how articles are retrieved by Internet search engines. So, it's worth spending time to create a title that conveys your work accurately. We suggest you avoid several genres of titles:

- *Titles that are too cute or too clever*: authors sometimes include the names of songs, television programs, or events from popular culture in their titles, usually followed by a more scientific-sounding phrase. The problem with this approach is that popular culture varies across geography and time. What may be a great example of popular culture in one country may be meaningless in another country and meaningless everywhere in a decade or so. If you want to engage the reader with a non-scientific phrase, proverbs (e.g., *A bird in the hand is better than two in the bush*) represent a better choice because they have, by definition, proven the test of time and are often common across cultures.
- *Titles that include "preliminary"*: some authors apparently think that adding "preliminary" may convince readers to use a lower bar for evaluating a manuscript. We're skeptical that this works. If a study is really preliminary (e.g., the sample is too small), use the findings to design a study that addresses the issue at hand, but don't try to publish the preliminary findings.
- *Titles of the form "the relationships between variables X, Y, and Z"*: undergraduates (at least in the United States) often use this kind of title for their research, so it tends to make your work seem unsophisticated. More important, sociologists are not typically interested in variables per se; instead, they're interested in relationships among constructs that such variables represent.

Instead of these kinds of titles, we encourage titles that describe the results of your work. Here are two examples: "Volunteering is linked to less cognitive decline, especially for women" and "Higher education liberalizes moral concerns, especially for students who major in the humanities, arts, and social sciences." Both titles are succinct summaries of the main findings reported in the article.

Of course, sometimes a study's key results are too complex to be summarized neatly in a single, concise sentence. In this case, we suggest a title that mentions the key constructs from the study. Examples include "Schooling, socioeconomic inequality, and achievement" or "Cross-national comparisons of links between immigration and welfare spending."

You don't need to spend hours perfecting a title (e.g., trying to find the ideal proverb), but it should be more than an afterthought. A good title will appeal to readers and search engines alike, increasing the impact of the work you report.

Abstract

A good title grabs your reader's attention, but a well-written abstract sustains it. Abstracts in sociology journals include a variety of styles, but often consist of a single paragraph that includes one to two sentences about the background (or problem), hypotheses, methods, results, and conclusions. In writing the abstract, be sure to review the relevant journal's guidelines (these frequently include specific expectations for the abstract) and look at recent examples of published papers in that journal to get a sense of what the formatting should be. After that, we suggest the following strategies:

- write two to three sentences for each of the components of the abstract (e.g., background, methods) and then use the tips in Lesson 3 to pare this draft down to the specified number of words;
- be sure the writing is clear and nontechnical, particularly regarding the reasons why your results represent a substantial advance in scientific understanding; and
- write it after the rest of the manuscript is finished, so you know what the paper says!

Method

A method section describes how you conducted the study, in sufficient detail such that others could replicate your work. We often describe it to students as being analogous to a recipe: if people had the same ingredients (subjects or data), and they followed the recipe (described in the methods section), they would produce a meal that tastes the same (would yield the same results). Writing a method section is straightforward and all about details, with little room for creativity or most of the tips described earlier in this book. For that reason, we usually turn to the method section when we're having difficulty writing a more important part of the manuscript—it requires comparatively little brainpower. As you write this section, we urge you to

- use subheadings generously, starting with the mandatory (e.g., "Dependent Variable" and "Analysis Plan" for quantitative work) but adding others as necessary;

- avoid abbreviations and instead use descriptive terms for conditions, groups, and names of variables;
- provide as much information as possible about the participants in your study (e.g., "the sample included 802 people" won't do!);
- describe what participants in the study actually did, not what they were asked to do (e.g., not "Participants were then asked to rate their health on a five-point Likert item ..." but "Participants rated their health on five-point Likert item ..."); and
- upload copies of all materials (e.g., stimuli, questionnaires) to the journal's website as supplementary material to be published online only.

From Principles to Practices

Maybe you're eager to use the tips we've described on your next writing project but there seem to be so many! It's overwhelming to remember all of them and to know when to use each one. Relax. Take several deep breaths. In the next few pages, we'll suggests how to make these tips "your own"—tools that you "automatically" use while writing.

Practice, Practice, Practice

Writing is a skill, not an innate talent: mastering the tools we've described requires lots of practice. Lots! If you've completed the exercises in the book, you've taken the first steps to mastering the tools. But, for novice writers, the practice you've gotten here just gets you to the base of Mt. Effective Writing: you have a long way to climb before you can see the summit. And for most writers, reaching the summit is a life-long aim. But we are confident that if you practice regularly, it is a summit you can reach!

We encourage you to use to complete the "For Practice" items that appear at the end of every lesson. We suggest that you set aside 15–20 minutes each week and devote that time for the "For Practice" items in one chapter. In the next week, move to the items in the next chapter; in just under seven weeks, you will have gone through all seven lessons. Then repeat this cycle; in about four months (the length of a semester), you will have considered each of the lessons twice and the tips will start to become more automatic. (This is especially likely if you practice regularly with one or two other writers and compare your answers.)

These Are Tips, Not Rules; Feel Free to Use Some Tips but Not Others

Some of the tips we've described may appeal more or be more useful to you than others. Cool: use them and ignore the others. What we've described are not rules that should be applied dogmatically; instead think of them as practical guides—guides that are useful for many writers much of the time. But not for everyone and not always.

Some of these tips can be contentious. For example, many students are taught to avoid passive voice and, instead, to always use active voice. We agree that active voice is usually best, but passive voice is occasionally the most effective way to communicate. For example, we saw in Lesson 4 that passive voice allows writers to start a sentence with familiar information, a key strategy for creating flow within a paragraph.

If a person evaluating your manuscript objects in principle to one of the tips that you've used, we suggest that you try to convince them otherwise. (Maybe by suggesting that they read this book!) But if this person can't be convinced *and* is giving you a grade or deciding whether your paper should be published, concede the point. However, if the person doesn't have that power over the fate of your paper, then feel free to ignore suggestions regarding arbitrary grammatical rules (e.g., "never start a sentence with 'however'") that don't make your writing clearer.

Create a Process for Writing

Our guidelines are more effective when applied systematically, not haphazardly. This means that you need a writing process. Just as you're more likely to master a musical instrument if you have routines for practicing and performing, you'll be more successful if you have a process for writing. Many authors have described how to create productive writing habits (e.g., King, 2010; Lambert, 2013; Silva, 2019). They identify several key ingredients in a successful writing process:

- *Try to write regularly and frequently.* Many students and faculty members tend to wait until they have a big chunk of time to work on a writing project, and then try to write a huge amount in a quick sprint to the finish. Although some writers have success with this approach, for most writers, a more effective approach is to schedule writing time most days. If your schedule doesn't allow you to write every day, try to write at least a couple of times a week. Not only does regular writing keep you in the flow of your writing projects, it gives you regular practice at writing. And, like any craft, regular practice is a key to being a great writer.

- *Never give in to "writer's block!"* If you don't know where to start, simply write on the page "I'm stuck, and I can't figure out where to begin." If that doesn't get the words flowing, write the reasons that you can't figure out where to begin. Soon, you are going to start filling up your pages with metawriting (i.e., writing about writing). Even though the metawriting typically won't remain in the manuscript, this process gets you thinking about writing enough that you will begin to clarify your thoughts and thus pave the way for your "real" writing.

- *Expect your rough draft to be rough; get it into shape by revising.* The rough draft is a way for you to get all your ideas on the page in a way that makes sense to you. As you write a rough draft, avoid editing and making corrections; save that for the next step: revising. During revising, use the tips from the seven lessons to present the words in a way that the ideas that make sense to you also make sense to the reader.

- *Expect your writing process to be non-linear.* Some writers start writing at the introduction, write linearly until they get to the conclusion, then do some quick revising. This rarely yields the best manuscript. Instead, feel free to tackle the different sections of a manuscript in any order that you like. For example, some writers prefer to begin with the results (because they consider it the most important section to "get right"); others, with the method (because it's often the easiest to write and so it's a good starting point). As you revise, expect that changes in one section may force changes in another. For example, as you develop an idea fully in the discussion, you may need to say more about it in the introduction. Finally, be willing to recognize when your approach to a topic isn't working and that you need to abandon it for another. In this way, writing is not so much like a nonstop flight from start to finish but more like a road trip in which your progress to the destination is filled with deviations, back-tracking, and the occasional traffic jam.

- *Know when to let go.* Work hard and revise extensively to get your work to a good place, and then get it out the door to get some feedback. Ask friends or colleagues for their comments. But don't fuss endlessly trying to be sure that everything is perfect, because that's an unattainable goal. Trust your efforts and get your work out for others to read.

Thanks for reading our book and for allowing us to join you in your writing journey. As you continue your journey, you'll have setbacks and make some "mistakes" (rather than "mistakes," we prefer to think of these as "suboptimal writing"). Don't let these discourage you; learn from them, celebrate your writing wins, and, most important, enjoy the journey; take pride in each step forward in your writing. And, let us know how you're doing; we'd love to hear from you.

Finally, when it comes to writing for sociology, remember that it isn't about how many words you write, it isn't about how good you think your writing is, it isn't about how many people you can impress, it isn't about all the money you'll (probably not) make, and it isn't about fame or glory: it's about communicating to your reader in a way that is clear and concise.

Glossary

Adverbial clause—a dependent clause that modifies a verb, adjective, or adverb.
My son told me another fight broke out *where he eats lunch at school*.

Antimetabole—a figure of speech in which emphasis is created by repeating words within a clause but in the reverse order.
These findings indicate that when people love to cheat, they may cheat on those they love.

Dependent clause—a group of words that includes a subject and a verb but that cannot stand alone as a complete sentence; also known as a subordinate clause.
Although these results contradict previous findings in the literature, our view is that the contradiction is more apparent than real.

Hedge—a word (typically an adverb, adjective, or verb) used to convey caution.
This evidence *seems* to lead to the conclusion that ...

Hyperbole—a figure of speech in which an exaggerated statement is used for emphasis; not recommended for scientific writing because readers may interpret the statement literally.
The literature on racism is filled with billions of studies.

Independent clause—a group of words that includes a subject and a verb and that can stand alone as a complete sentence; also known as a main clause.
Although these results seem to contradict previous findings in the literature, *our view is that the contradiction is more apparent than real*.

Intensifier—a word (typically an adverb, adjective, or verb) used to convey emphasis.
This evidence *clearly* leads to the conclusion that ...

Metaphor—a figure of speech in which two dissimilar things are compared implicitly.
For individuals who are depressed, occasional happy experiences *drown in a sea of negative affect*.

Neologism—a new word, often created by adding prefixes or suffixes, using hyperhyphenated modifiers, or by verbing.
Instagramaholic (adding a suffix); *relying-on-hyphens-to-add-spice author* (hyperhyphenated modifier), *Last week we zoomed* (from the noun *Zoom*).

Nominalization—a noun derived from a verb or adjective.
Significance (from the adjective *significant*), *personification* (from the verb *personify*).

Passive voice—a grammatical construction in which the subject of the sentence is a noun that would be the object in a sentence written in active voice.
Longitudinal studies have been conducted by sociologists to determine whether ... (The noun phrase *longitudinal studies* is the object of the verb *have been conducted*.)

Periodic sentence—a sentence that begins with a long, dependent clause in which one word is repeated several times and ends with the independent clause; typically used for emphasis.
Without food, *without* water, *without* shelter, *without* clothing, and *without* money, the refugees were desperate.

Relative pronoun—a pronoun used to introduce a dependent clause; *that, which, who, whom,* and *whose* are common examples.
This finding was unexpected and suggests *that* previous findings may be spurious.

Simile—a figure of speech in which two dissimilar things are compared explicitly, using *like* or *as*.
For overworked employees, satisfying homelife is like a haven from stormy work life.

Topic sentence—a sentence that is usually the first sentence in a paragraph and introduces the idea of the paragraph by including a topic and a controlling idea about that topic.
Individuals with low self-control are more likely to make sacrifices for their spouses and partners. (topic = individuals with low self-control; controlling idea = they are more likely to make sacrifices for their spouses and partners)

Understatement—a figure of speech in which a description is deliberately less strong than the facts or conditions warrant; not recommended for scientific writing because readers may interpret the statement literally.
Women were paid somewhat less than men.
Would illustrate understatement if women were paid 50% less.

Verbing—a technique to add spice to writing by creating a new verb from a noun.
I'll photoshop the picture later (from *Photoshop*); *zoomed* (from *Zoom*).

Bibliography

Allport, G. W. (1954). *The nature of prejudice*. Addison-Wesley.

Daniels, N. (2021, February 21). What students are saying about race and racism in America. *The New York Times*. Retrieved from https://www.nytimes.com/2021/02/18/learning/what-students-are-saying-about-race-and-racism-in-america.html.

Drehs, W. (2020, May 18). Michael Phelps: 'This is the most overwhelmed I've ever felt'. *ESPN*. Retrieved from https://www.espn.com/olympics/story/_/id/29186389/michael-phelps-most-overwhelmed-ever-felt.

Dupuis-Panther, F. (n.d.). Sandra Hempel: An interview with the guitar player. *Jazz Halo*. Retrieved from https://www.jazzhalo.be/interviews/sandra-hempel-an-interview-with-the-guitar-player/.

Ehrenclou, M. (2019, April 9). Interview with Ana Popovic, guitar slinger, singer-songwriter. *Rock and Blues Muse*. Retrieved from https://www.rockandbluesmuse.com/2019/04/09/interview-with-ana-popovic-guitar-slinger-singer-songwriter/.

Female Rockers. (2000, December). Interview with Mary N. *Female Rockers*. Retrieved from https://femalerockers.com/maryn.

Gleeson, S., & Brady, E. (2017, August 30). When athletes share their battles with mental illness. *USA TODAY*. Retrieved from https://www.usatoday.com/story/sports/2017/08/30/michael-phelps-brandon-marshall-mental-health-battles-royce-white-jerry-west/596857001/.

Hillman, K. (2021, June 25). Mother and teen reflect on the pride and joy of growing up transgender. [Radio Broadcast]. NPR. Retrieved from https://storycorps.org/stories/mother-and-teen-reflect-on-the-pride-and-joy-of-growing-up-transgender/.

Irwin, V., Zhang, J., Wang, X., Hein, S., Wang, K., Roberts, A., York, C., Barmer, A., Bullock Mann, F., Dilig, R., & Parker, S. (2021). *Report on the condition of education 2021* (NCES 2021-144). U.S. Department of Education. Washington, DC: National Center for Education Statistics.

Kearl, H. (2018). The facts behind the #metoo movement: A national study on sexual harassment and assault. *Stop Street Harassment*. Retrieved from https://www.nsvrc.org/sites/default/files/2021-04/full-report-2018-national-study-on-sexual-harassment-and-assault.pdf.

Kendall, P. C., Silk, J. S., & Chu, B. C. (2000). Introducing your research report: Writing the introduction. In R. J. Sternberg (Ed.), *Guide to publishing in psychology journals* (pp. 41–57). Cambridge: Cambridge University Press.

King, M. L. (1994). *Letter from the Birmingham jail*. San Francisco, CA: Harper San Francisco.

King, S. (2010). *On writing: A memoir of the craft*. New York: Scribner.

Lambert, N. M. (2013). *Publish and prosper: A strategy guide for students and researchers*. Hoboken, NJ: Taylor and Francis.

Plotnik, A. (2007). *Spunk and bite: A writer's guide to bold, contemporary style*. New York: Random House Reference.

Silvia, P. J. (2019). *How to write a lot: A practical guide to productive academic writing*. Washington, DC: American Psychological Association.

Van Amburg, J. (2016, October 21). Abby Wambach on her addiction struggle. 'I Felt like a fraud'. *Time*. Retrieved from https://time.com/4518626/abby-wambach-addiction-dui-together-tour/.

Williams, J. M. (2000). *Style: Ten lessons in clarity and grace* (6th ed.). New York: Longman.

Index

Printed in the United States
by Baker & Taylor Publisher Services